i Can Speak
3 Blue
An integrated course for communicative success

Pagoda Language Education Center

PAGODA Books

Copyright © 2011 by PAGODA Books

All rights reserved. No part of this publication may be reproduced, stored in a retrieval system, or transmitted, in any form, or by any means, electronic, mechanical, photocopying, recording or otherwise, without the prior written permission of the copyright holder and the publisher.

Published by PAGODA Books
PAGODA Books is the professional language publishing company of the PAGODA Education Group.
19F, PAGODA Tower, 419, Gangnam-daero,
Seocho-gu, Seoul, 06614, Rep. of KOREA
www.pagodabook.com

First published 2011
Fifteenth impression 2025
Printed in the Republic of Korea

ISBN 978-89-6281-248-0 (14740)

Publisher | Kyung-Sil Park
Writer | PAGODA Language Education Center

Acknowledgements

Thanks to the following for their contribution in providing us with feedback:
Sue Ahn, Ahmi Cha, Jessica Han, Cindy Jung, Amber Kang, Ella Kim, Grace Kim, Christina Lee, Joanne Lee, Kacey Lee, Kay Lim, Mia Lim, Sooji Park, Rachel Shin, Rose Shin

A defective book may be exchanged at the store where you purchased it.

Introduction

What is *i* Can Speak?

i Can Speak is a three-level, six-book series designed to develop English speaking skills. Levels 1 through 3 cover the elementary, pre-intermediate, and intermediate levels, respectively. The books focus on real-life communication, presenting learners with realistic scenarios and engaging, relevant activities. Aside from developing speaking skills, *i* Can Speak 3 Blue also includes reading, writing, and listening activities to help intermediate students become all-round communicators.

How is the book organized?

Each lesson includes:

- A **Warm-Up** activity, which activates learners' knowledge of the lesson's theme and gets the class talking straight away
- Two **dialogues**, which present the lesson's theme and language points within real-life contexts
- **Language Focus** boxes, which highlight key language from dialogues for learners to use in the following speaking activities
- Three graded **Talk** speaking activities, which allow learners to practice and personalize the lesson's language focus. Some **Talk** activities also include listening practice.
- *i* **Read** – an opportunity for learners to react to written stimulus based on the lesson's theme
- *i* **Write** – an activity that gives learners the chance to express themselves in writing, using the lesson's theme and language focus

What is included with the book?

The book is accompanied by:

- An **audio CD** containing all the listening material from the book
- A **Mini Book**, which includes the dialogues and pronunciation material from each lesson, as well as a Wordlist for every lesson
- **MP3 files** downloadable from www.pagodabook.com

Scope and Sequence

Introduction — 3
Key to Phonetic Symbols — 6
Table of Irregular Verbs — 7
Classroom Language — 8

	Theme	Language Focus	Page
Lesson 1 The disadvantage of Mexico is that it's too hot.	Vacations 1	• Advantages and Disadvantages • Fears	10
Lesson 2 May I see your passport, please?	Travel Practicalities	• Airport Immigration • Hotels	18
Lesson 3 I'd like to rent a vehicle, please.	Traveling in a Foreign Country	• Renting a Vehicle • Giving Advice about Customs	26
Lesson 4 What's your major?	Education	• Talking about Studies	34
Lesson 5 Do you want to live alone, or in a shared apartment?	Finding a Place to Live	• Talking with Letting Agents • Comparing Cities	42
Lesson 6 That's quite a personal question.	Difficult People	• Personal Questions 1 • Personal Questions 2	50
Lesson 7 What kind of treatment did you get?	Health	• Talking about Health 1 • Talking about Health 2	58
Lesson 8 What is an American wedding like?	Wedding Customs	• Weddings 1 • Weddings 2	66

	Theme	Language Focus	Page
Lesson 9 **I ran a red light.**	Crime	• Traffic Offenses • Talking about Robbery	74
Lesson 10 **What's your emergency?**	Emergencies	• Emergencies 1 • Emergencies 2	82
Lesson 11 **What kind of job are you interested in?**	Job Hunting	• Talking about Jobs • Talking about Work Experience	90
Lesson 12 **What do you enjoy about your job?**	At Work	• Talking about Likes and Dislikes • Discussing Problems at Work	98
Lesson 13 **I want to go somewhere special.**	Vacations 2	• Expressing Interest • Talking about Vacations	106
Lesson 14 **I downloaded some apps for my smartphone.**	Technology	• Explaining How to Use Technology • Persuading • Rejecting Persuasion	114
Lesson 15 **I'm against the idea.**	For and Against	• Discussing Opinions • Discussing Ideas	122
Lesson 16 **I'd probably ask him for his autograph.**	Hopes and Dreams	• Imagined Situations • Hopes and Dreams	130

Listening Scripts ---- 138

Key to Phonetic Symbols

Consonants

/p/	park	/ŋ/	sing	/z/	rise
/t/	time	/f/	laugh	/ʒ/	vision
/k/	cat	/θ/	thing	/dʒ/	page
/b/	rob	/s/	rice	/w/	want
/d/	road	/ʃ/	action	/r/	ride
/g/	go	/tʃ/	church	/l/	live
/m/	make	/v/	very	/j/	use
/n/	rain	/ð/	those	/h/	here

Vowels

/ɪ/	sit	/e/	any	/ɑ/	on	/ɔɪ/	boy
/iː/	seat	/ɜː/	early	/ɑː/	arm	/eə/	area
/uː/	you	/ɔː/	sport	/ɪə/	near	/əʊ/	over
/ə/	arrive	/æ/	apple	/ʊə/	tour	/aɪ/	eye
/ʊ/	good	/ʌ/	umbrella	/eɪ/	face	/aʊ/	cow

Table of Irregular Verbs

Base Form	Simple Past	Past Participle	Base Form	Simple Past	Past Participle
be	was/were	been	let	let	let
beat	beat	beaten	lie	lay	lain
become	became	become	light	lit	lit
begin	began	begun	lose	lost	lost
bite	bit	bitten	make	made	made
blow	blew	blown	mean	meant	meant
break	broke	broken	meet	met	met
bring	brought	brought	pay	paid	paid
build	built	built	put	put	put
buy	bought	bought	read	read	read
catch	caught	caught	ride	rode	ridden
choose	chose	chosen	ring	rang	rung
come	came	come	rise	rose	risen
cost	cost	cost	run	ran	run
cut	cut	cut	say	said	said
do	did	done	see	saw	seen
draw	drew	drawn	sell	sold	sold
drink	drank	drunk	send	sent	sent
drive	drove	driven	shine	shone	shone
eat	ate	eaten	shoot	shot	shot
fall	fell	fallen	show	showed	shown/showed
feel	felt	felt	shut	shut	shut
fight	fought	fought	sing	sang	sung
find	found	found	sit	sat	sat
fly	flew	flown	sleep	slept	slept
forget	forgot	forgotten	speak	spoke	spoken
get	got	gotten	spend	spent	spent
give	gave	given	stand	stood	stood
go	went	gone	steal	stole	stolen
grow	grew	grown	swim	swam	swum
hang	hung	hung	take	took	taken
have	had	had	teach	taught	taught
hear	heard	heard	tear	tore	torn
hide	hid	hidden	tell	told	told
hit	hit	hit	think	thought	thought
hold	held	held	throw	threw	thrown
hurt	hurt	hurt	understand	understood	understood
keep	kept	kept	wake	woke	woken
know	knew	known	wear	wore	worn
leave	left	left	win	won	won
lend	lent	lent	write	wrote	written

Classroom Language

Teacher Talk

Student Talk

Lesson 1
The disadvantage of Mexico is that it's too hot.

Warm-Up

A Work in two groups. Decide which form of transportation is the best. Give reasons for your decision.

tour bus

cruise ship

train

car

bicycle

airplane

B Tell the class what you decided and why.

Dialogue 1 — Listen to the dialogue and practice.

Travel agent:	How can I help you today?
Gina:	We'd like to book a vacation.
Travel agent:	OK. Where would you like to go?
Gina:	We'd like to go somewhere quiet and warm.
Simon:	Yes, and somewhere with a good beach.
Travel agent:	Perhaps Mexico would be a good destination for you.
Gina:	Hmm … the disadvantage of Mexico is that it's too hot.
Simon:	Yes, we like warm weather, but not hot weather.
Travel agent:	Then how about Florida? A major advantage of Florida is that you can travel there by train. You don't need to fly.
Gina:	I think we'd like to go somewhere further away than Florida. We want to go somewhere interesting with lots of things to do, and—
Simon:	And, somewhere not too expensive.
Travel agent:	OK. Let me take a look at our database and see what we have.

Comprehension Check!

1. What kind of place do Gina and Simon want to go to for vacation?
2. What do they say about Mexico and Florida?

Language Focus 1

Advantages and Disadvantages

The/A (main/big/great) disadvantage of Mexico is (that) it's too hot.

The/A/An (major/big/great) advantage of Florida is (that) you can travel there by train.

Another advantage/disadvantage (of Mexico**) is (that)** it's far away.

Florida is warm. Mexico, **on the other hand**, is hot.

Talk 1

A Decide with your partner which of the tourist destinations is best for Gina and Simon from **Dialogue 1**. Give reasons for your decisions.

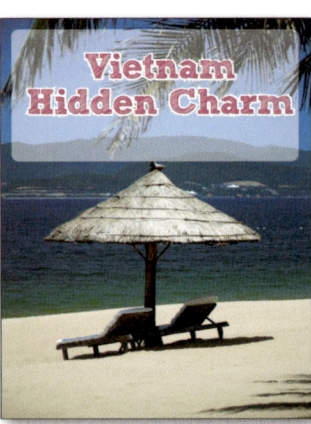

B Discuss with your partner the advantages and disadvantages of the tourist destinations in **A**. Which place would you choose for a vacation? Why?

> Example
>
> **A:** I think the main advantage of Rome is that there are lots of monuments.
> **B:** That's true. Another advantage is that the food there is delicious.
> **A:** You're right. What do you think are the disadvantages of Rome?
>
>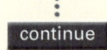

Pronunciation

Syllables

Discover Pronunciation!
English words are made of smaller sounds called *syllables*. Look at the words from **Dialogue 1**:

Help = one syllable
Today = two syllables
Vacation = three syllables

Practice Pronunciation!

A Read the sentences from **Dialogue 1**. How many syllables are there in each sentence? Listen to check your answers.

1. How can I help you today? 7
2. We'd like to book a vacation.
3. Perhaps Mexico would be a good destination for you.
4. The disadvantage of Mexico is that it's too hot.
5. A major advantage of Florida is that you can travel there by train.

B Practice saying the sentences in **A**. Pay attention to the number of syllables.

Talk 2

A Discuss with your partner the advantages and disadvantages of your country as a tourist destination. Write five advantages and five disadvantages.

Advantages	Disadvantages
1.	1.
2.	2.
3.	3.
4.	4.
5.	5.

B Tell the class about the advantages and disadvantages you wrote in **A**. Do your classmates agree with you?

Example
We felt that the main advantage of our country is that there are lots of places for tourists to visit. Also, ...

Dialogue 2 — Listen to the dialogue and practice.

Isabel: Do you like flying?
William: No, not at all. It makes me nervous. What about you?
Isabel: I feel the same way as you. People often say that flying is safer than driving, but I know which I'd prefer!
William: Yes, I agree. I always worry about bad weather. I hate it when there's a lot of turbulence. It makes me feel sick.
Isabel: I know what you mean. I also worry about missing my flight, or losing my luggage.
William: Yes, I've lost my luggage a few times.
Isabel: My worst fear is that the plane will crash, or be hijacked. What's your worst fear?
William: It's the height that scares me the most. I wish I wasn't sitting next to the window!
Isabel: Shall we switch seats, then?
William: That'd be great. Thanks!

Comprehension Check!

1. Do Isabel and William like flying?
2. What are their worst fears?

Language Focus 2

Fears	
Do you like flying?	Yes, I like it.
	No, not at all. It makes me nervous/scared.
Are you scared of flying?	Yes, I am. / Yes, kind of. / No, I'm not.
	I don't mind it.
	Actually, I like it.
What are you scared of?	**I (always) worry about** bad weather.
What are your fears?	**I hate it when** there's a lot of turbulence. It makes me feel sick.
What's your worst/biggest fear?	**My worst fear is that** the plane **will** crash.
	It's the height **that scares me the most**.
	I'm most scared of heights.

Talk 3

 A What are you scared of? Discuss your fears with your partner, referring to the pictures.

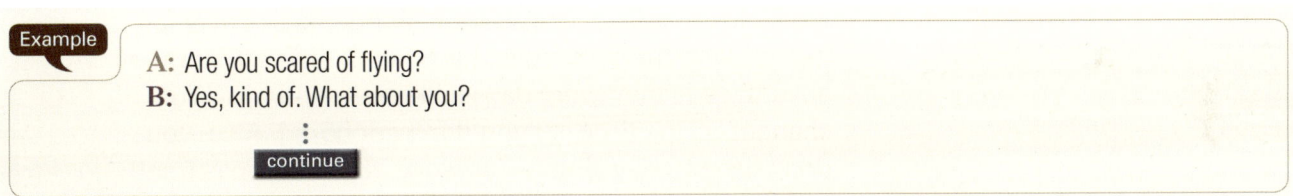

A: Are you scared of flying?
B: Yes, kind of. What about you?
⋮
continue

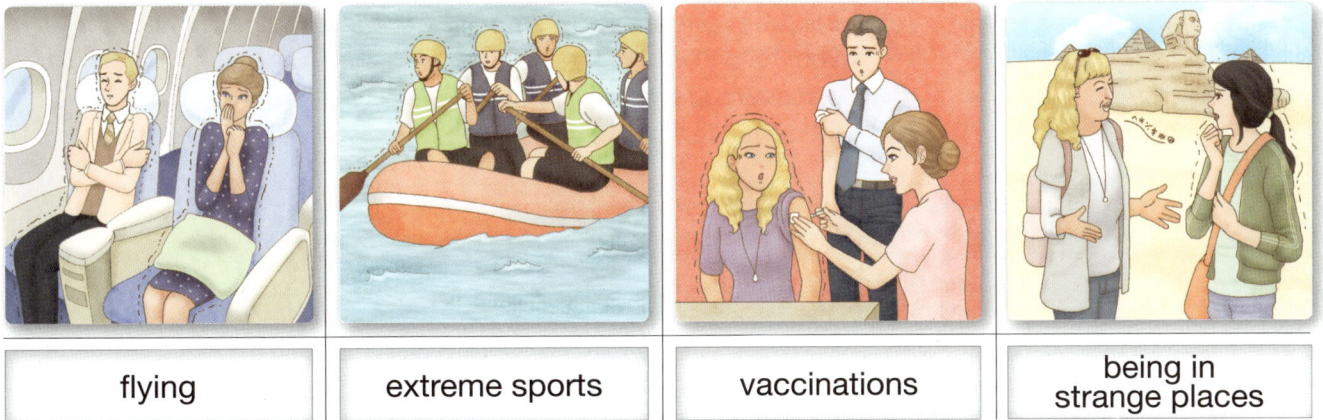

| flying | extreme sports | vaccinations | being in strange places |

B Tell your partner about a time when you were scared. Refer to the questions.

1. What were you scared of?
2. What happened?
3. How did you feel?

i Read

A Read the discussion from an internet forum. What job is rachel-air interested in?

---

15 June, 09:20 am #1

rachel-air
Junior Member
Join Date: Jun 2011
Posts: 3

What are the advantages and disadvantages of being a flight attendant?

I'm interested in becoming a flight attendant. What are the advantages and disadvantages of this job? I'd love to hear your opinions. Thanks xx

---

15 June, 10:02 am #2

cieloazul
Full Member
Join Date: Mar 2009
Posts: 43

What are the advantages and disadvantages of being a flight attendant?

The big advantage of being a flight attendant is the free travel. Most airlines allow flight attendants to travel for free, or extremely cheaply, during their time off. Another advantage is that every day is different. Your schedule changes all the time, so you don't get bored. Also, you don't have to buy clothes for work. The uniform is free!

The main disadvantage of being a flight attendant is that the job is physically and mentally challenging. Sometimes you have to work for 12–14 hours in the air. Another disadvantage is that it is difficult to have a family or love life because you are away from home so often.

B Discuss the questions with your partner.

1. According to the writer, what are the advantages of the job?
2. According to the writer, what are the disadvantages of the job?
3. Can you think of any other advantages/disadvantages?
4. Would you like to have the job?

i Write

A Choose one of the jobs and brainstorm the advantages and disadvantages.

Job:

Advantages	Disadvantages

B Write about the advantages and disadvantages of the job you chose in **A**.

Lesson 1 · 17

Lesson 2
May I see your passport, please?

Warm-Up

A Match the types of accommodation with the pictures.

motel   youth hostel   inn   hotel   camping park   homestay   lodge

B Which of the types of accommodation in **A** have you stayed in? Tell the class about your experiences.

Dialogue 1 — Listen to the dialogue and practice.

Officer: Welcome to Australia. May I see your passport, please?
Francesca: Yes. Here it is.
Officer: What is the purpose of your visit to Australia?
Francesca: I've come to study. I have a student visa.
Officer: So I see. And how long do you plan to stay?
Francesca: For one year.
Officer: Where will you be living?
Francesca: I'll be living in homestay accommodation with a host family.
Officer: I see. How are you going to get to your homestay from the airport?
Francesca: My school is picking me up.
Officer: OK. Enjoy your stay!
Francesca: Thank you.

Comprehension Check!

1. Where are the speakers?
2. What does Francesca plan to do? Where will she live?

Language Focus 1

Airport Immigration

May I see your passport, please? Could I see your passport? Show me your passport, please.	Here it is. Of course. Sure.
What is the purpose of your visit/trip?	I've come to study / to visit relatives / to visit friends. I'm here on business/vacation.
How long do you plan to stay? How long will you be staying? How long will you be here?	(I'll be staying / I'll be here) For two weeks / one month / one year.
Where will you be living/staying?	(I'll be staying/living) At a hotel / In homestay accommodation / With a host family / With friends / With relatives.
How are you going to get to your accommodation from the airport? How are you going to travel from the airport?	My relative/friend/school is picking me up. I'm going to take a taxi/bus. I'm taking the subway.

Talk 1

Work in groups of five. Roleplay conversations between an immigration officer and four travelers at an airport. Refer to the landing cards.

Example
A: Welcome to Australia. Show me your passport, please.
B: Here it is.
A: What is the purpose of your trip?
continue

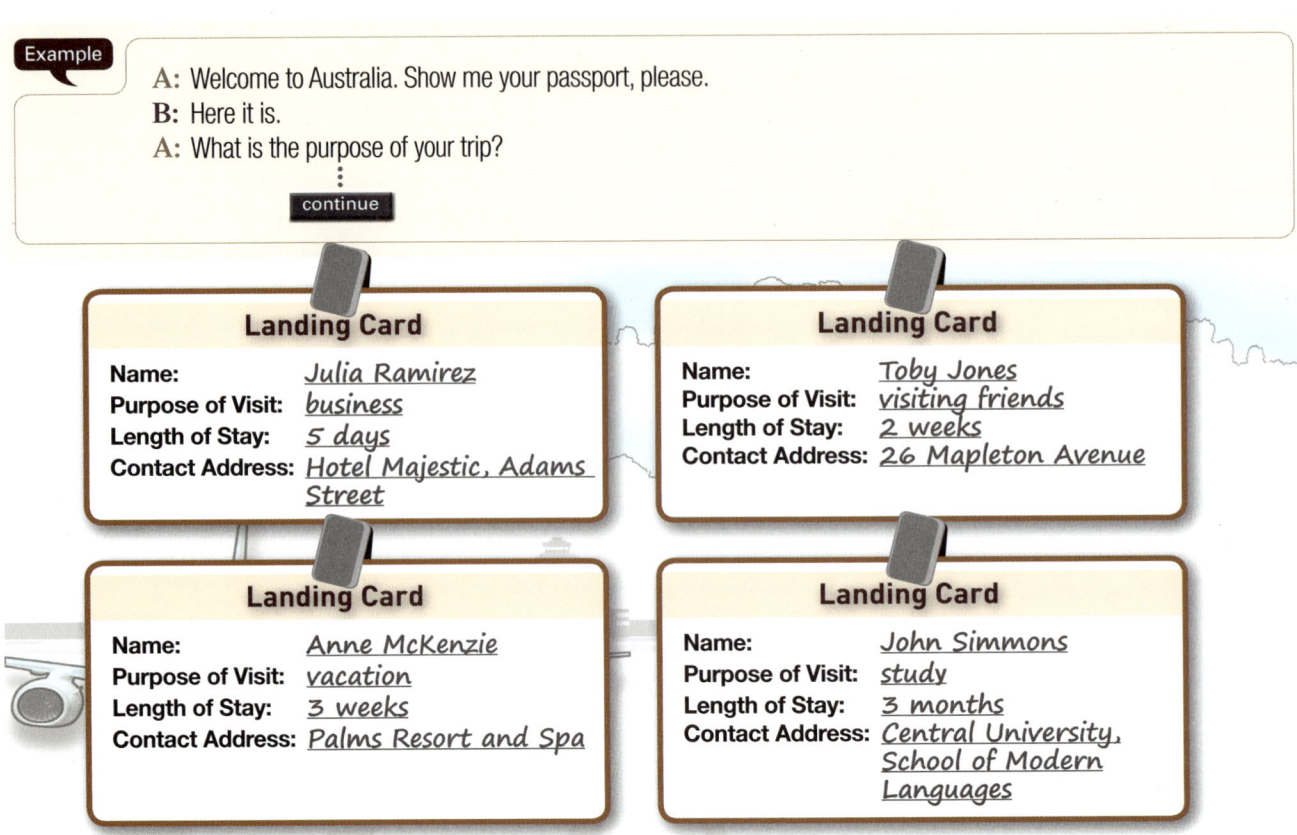

Landing Card
Name: Julia Ramirez
Purpose of Visit: business
Length of Stay: 5 days
Contact Address: Hotel Majestic, Adams Street

Landing Card
Name: Toby Jones
Purpose of Visit: visiting friends
Length of Stay: 2 weeks
Contact Address: 26 Mapleton Avenue

Landing Card
Name: Anne McKenzie
Purpose of Visit: vacation
Length of Stay: 3 weeks
Contact Address: Palms Resort and Spa

Landing Card
Name: John Simmons
Purpose of Visit: study
Length of Stay: 3 months
Contact Address: Central University, School of Modern Languages

Dialogue 2 — Listen to the dialogue and practice.

Receptionist: Good morning. How can I help you?
Camilla: I'd like a single room. Do you have any vacancies?
Receptionist: Yes, we do. How long would you like to stay?
Camilla: Three nights. How much is a single room?
Receptionist: 150 dollars a night, and we ask for the full amount in advance. The price includes complimentary breakfast. Breakfast is served in the lobby between 7:30 am and 10 am.
Camilla: OK, I'll take it. Is it too early to check in?
Receptionist: I'm afraid you can't check in until 4 pm. We can look after your luggage for you until then, though.
Camilla: OK, that would be great. Thanks.
Receptionist: No problem. Now, if you could give me a credit card, I'll book you in.

Comprehension Check!

1. How long does Camilla want to stay in the hotel?
2. What kind of room does Camilla want? Why does she have to wait until 4 pm?

Language Focus 2

Hotels	
How can I help you? May I help you?	We'd like a double room / single room / suite. Do you have any vacancies? Are you fully booked?
How long would you like to stay? How long will you be staying with us?	Two nights/weeks. **Until** Wednesday.
Does the price include breakfast?	Yes, it does. No, it doesn't.
What time is breakfast served? Where is breakfast served?	Breakfast is served in the lobby between 7:30 am and 10 am.
Is there a gym/restaurant/bar?	Yes, there is. No, I'm afraid there isn't.
Is it too early to check in?	No, you can check in now. Yes, I'm afraid you can't check in **until** 4 pm.
Can I get a wake-up call?	Of course. What time would you like it for?

Talk 2

A Match the hotel rooms and furnishings with the definitions.

1. a single room
2. a double room
3. a suite
4. a single bed
5. a double bed
6. twin beds

a. two single beds in one room
b. a bed for one person
c. a room for two or more people
d. a room for one person
e. a bed for two people
f. a set of connected rooms

B Decide with your partner which of the rooms and furnishings in **A** would be most suitable for each of the hotel guests. Give reasons for your decisions.

1. a large family
2. a couple
3. a businessperson
4. two businesspeople

Talk 3

Roleplay conversations between a hotel front desk receptionist and hotel guests. Refer to the information below.

Front Desk Receptionists

Central Palace

	Price	Available Rooms
Single	$120	☑
Double	$200	☐
Suite	$350	☑

Breakfast included ☐
Gym ☑
Restaurant ☑
Bar ☑
Pool ☐

The Rochester

	Price	Available Rooms
Single	$150	☐
Double	$230	☑
Suite	$400	☐

Breakfast included ☐
Gym ☑
Restaurant ☐
Bar ☐
Pool ☑

Metro Hotel

	Price	Available Rooms
Single	$90	☑
Double	$130	☑
Suite	$220	☑

Breakfast included ☑
Gym ☐
Restaurant ☐
Bar ☑
Pool ☑

Centennial Hotel

	Price	Available Rooms
Single	$80	☑
Double	$110	☑
Suite	$200	☐

Breakfast included ☐
Gym ☐
Restaurant ☑
Bar ☑
Pool ☑

Hotel Guests

Person 1   You are traveling with your sister. You need to stay for two nights. You want a hotel with a gym.

Person 2   You are traveling with your parents and grandparents. You need to stay for a week. You want a hotel with a restaurant.

Person 3   You are traveling alone. You need to stay for one night. You want a hotel with a bar.

Person 4   You are traveling with your wife/husband. You need to stay for three nights. You don't want to pay extra for breakfast.

Person 5   You are traveling with two friends. You need to stay for a week. You want a hotel with a pool.

Person 6   You are traveling alone. You need to stay for two nights. You want a hotel with a pool and a bar.

Example

A: Good morning. How can I help you?
B: I'd like a double room with twin beds. Do you have any vacancies?

i Read

A Read the e-mail from Jin-mi to her mother. What are Jin-mi's complaints about her homestay accommodation?

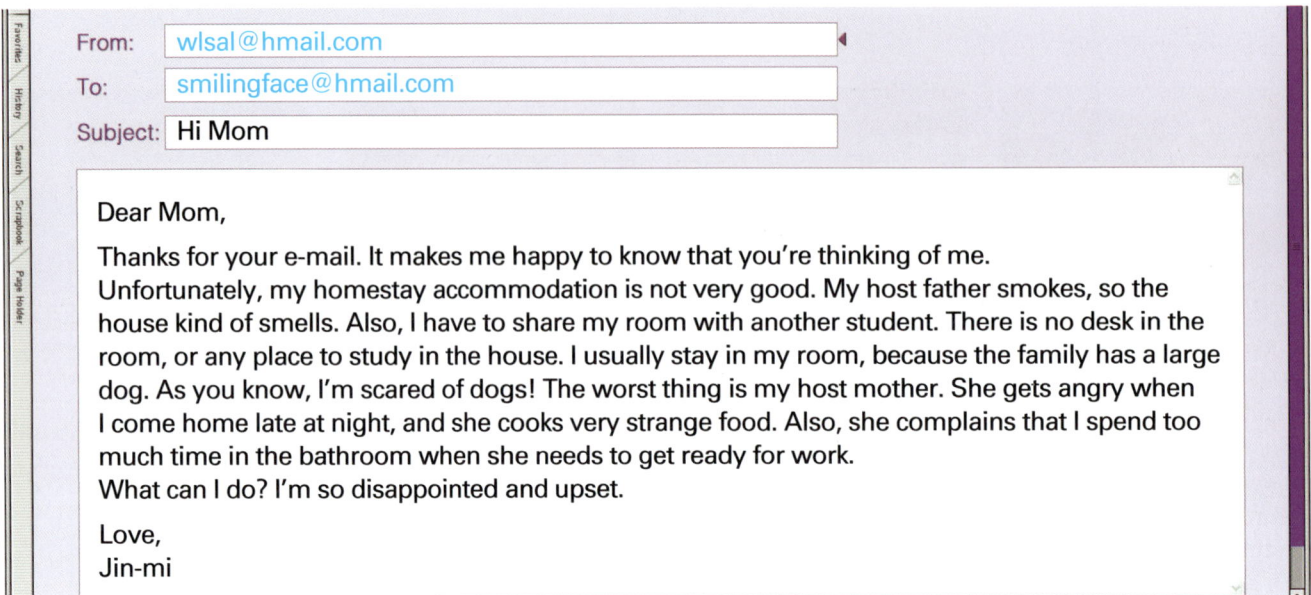

From: wlsal@hmail.com
To: smilingface@hmail.com
Subject: Hi Mom

Dear Mom,

Thanks for your e-mail. It makes me happy to know that you're thinking of me.
Unfortunately, my homestay accommodation is not very good. My host father smokes, so the house kind of smells. Also, I have to share my room with another student. There is no desk in the room, or any place to study in the house. I usually stay in my room, because the family has a large dog. As you know, I'm scared of dogs! The worst thing is my host mother. She gets angry when I come home late at night, and she cooks very strange food. Also, she complains that I spend too much time in the bathroom when she needs to get ready for work.
What can I do? I'm so disappointed and upset.

Love,
Jin-mi

B Discuss the questions with your partner.
1. What do you think about Jin-mi's complaints about her homestay accommodation?
2. What advice would you give to Jin-mi?
3. Have you ever lived in homestay accommodation? Tell the class about your experiences.

i Write

A Talk with your partner about what someone should/shouldn't do when living in homestay accommodation. Write your ideas.

Homestay Dos and Don'ts

Dos	Don'ts
✓	✗
✓	✗
✓	✗
✓	✗

B Write a reply to Jin-mi's e-mail in *i* **Read**. Give Jin-mi advice on living in her homestay accommodation.

Pronunciation

Identifying Word Stress

Discover Pronunciation!

Listen again to the words from the lesson. Notice the way the speakers stress different syllables in the words. Practice saying the words, paying attention to the stressed syllables.

●	●•	•●	●••	•●••	•••●•	••●••
host	purpose	amount	vacancies	Australia	accommodation	complimentary
stay	visit		family			
price	lobby					

When you learn a new word, it is useful to learn which syllable is stressed. This will help you pronounce the word correctly.

Practice Pronunciation!

A Complete the sentences with words from the table above. Listen to check your answers. Then match the stress patterns with the words.

1. I'm afraid we don't have any _____ at the moment.
2. The price includes _____ internet access.
3. Are you going to stay with a _____ family?
4. Let's meet in the _____ at nine o'clock.
5. We can pay the full _____ in advance.

a ●•
b •●
c ●
d ●••
e ••●••

B Practice saying the sentences in **A**. Pay attention to word stress.

Lesson 3 I'd like to rent a vehicle, please.

Warm-Up

A Match the words with the parts of the car.

- **a** hood
- **b** bumper
- **c** rearview mirror
- **d** headlight
- **e** license plate
- **f** gas tank door
- **g** windshield wiper
- **h** steering wheel
- **i** side mirror
- **j** tire

B Complete the sentences, using the appropriate words from the box.

| ticket | overtake | speed | pull | fine | slow |

1. When you reduce speed, you _____ down.
2. When you drive faster, you _____ up.
3. If you park in a place where parking is not allowed, you may get a parking _____ and a _____.
4. When you go past another car, you _____ it.
5. When you stop your car, you _____ over.

Dialogue 1 — Listen to the dialogue and practice.

Attendant: Good morning, Madam. What can I do for you?
Rebecca: Good morning. I'd like to rent a vehicle, please.
Attendant: Certainly. What kind of vehicle would you like to rent?
Rebecca: I'd like an SUV. We are a large family.
Attendant: OK. Let me see. Yes, we do have an SUV available. It's a Chevrolet Traverse. Is that OK for you?
Rebecca: Yes, that will be fine. How much will it be?
Attendant: The fee is 75 dollars a day. The price includes fully comprehensive insurance, and unlimited mileage. How many days would you like the vehicle for?
Rebecca: I need it for seven days.
Attendant: OK, I can book that in for you now. Could I see your driver's license, please?
Rebecca: Yes. Here you are.
Attendant: Thank you. I'll also need a credit card to make the booking.
Rebecca: No problem. Thanks.

Comprehension Check!

1. What kind of vehicle does Rebecca want to hire?
2. What does the attendant ask Rebecca to give him?

Language Focus 1

Renting a Vehicle	
What kind of vehicle would you like to rent?	I'd like to rent an SUV [= sports utility vehicle]. a four-door sedan a two-door coupe a station wagon a convertible a sports car a minivan a pickup truck a van
How much will it be?	The fee is 75 dollars a day. The price includes fully comprehensive insurance, and unlimited mileage.
How many days would you like the vehicle for?	I need it for seven days.
Could I see your driver's license, please?	Yes. Here you are.

Talk 1

A Match the vehicle names with the pictures.

- ⓐ convertible
- ⓑ station wagon
- ⓒ minivan
- ⓓ sports car
- ⓔ van
- ⓕ SUV
- ⓖ two-door coupe
- ⓗ four-door sedan
- ⓘ pickup truck

B Discuss the questions with your partner.

1. What kind of person drives each of the vehicles in **A**?
2. What kind of vehicles are the most popular in your country? Why?
3. What kind of vehicle would you like to own? Why?

Talk 2

Imagine that you want to rent one of the vehicles in **Talk 1**. Roleplay conversations with your partner.

> **Example**
> A: Good morning, sir. What can I do for you?
> B: Good morning. I'd like to rent a vehicle, please.
> A: Certainly. What kind of vehicle would you like to rent?
> ⋮
> continue

Dialogue 2 *Listen to the dialogue and practice.*

Harry: Hey, Tae-young. I hear you're going on vacation next month. Where are you going?
Tae-young: Yes, that's right. Actually, I'm going to your home country, the US!
Harry: Wow, great! Whereabouts are you going?
Tae-young: I'm going to the west coast with my husband. We're going to hire a car and drive to San Diego, Phoenix, and Las Vegas.
Harry: Sounds fantastic!
Tae-young: Yes. I can't wait! Do you have any tips for driving in the US?
Harry: Sure. Firstly, remember that there is a 15 mph speed limit near schools. Also, if a pedestrian steps onto a crosswalk, you must stop and let them cross. And don't park in a disabled space! If you do, you will get a large fine.
Tae-young: Wow! There is a lot to remember.
Harry: Yes! Also, if a police car follows you and flashes its lights, pull over as soon as possible.
Tae-young: And then? Get out of the car?
Harry: No, you shouldn't get out of the car. You will need to show your driver's license to the police officer.
Tae-young: OK. Any other tips?
Harry: Yes. Never drink and drive! That is a serious offense in the US.

Comprehension Check!

❶ What is Tae-young going to do next month?
❷ What six pieces of advice does Harry give Tae-young?

Language Focus 2

Giving Advice about Driving Customs

Firstly, **remember that** there is a 15 mph speed limit near schools.
If a pedestrian steps onto a crosswalk**, you must** stop and let them cross.
If a police car follows you and flashes its lights**, pull over** as soon as possible.
Don't park in a disabled space! **If you do, you will** get a large fine.
You shouldn't get out of the car.
You will need to show your driver's license to the police officer.
Never drink and drive!

Talk 3

 Talk with your partner about driving customs in your country. Write your ideas.

> Driving in my country
> •
> •
> •
> •

 Imagine that your partner is a visitor hiring a car in your country. Roleplay a conversation, using the information in **A**.

> Example
>
> **A:** Do you have any tips for driving in your country?
> **B:** Sure. Firstly, remember that the speed limit on highways is between 80 kph and 110 kph. Also, if ··· `continue`

 **Pronunciation**

Sentence Stress

Discover Pronunciation!

Listen to the extracts from **Dialogue 1** and **Dialogue 2**. Notice how the speaker stresses some words more than other words.

I'd like to rent a vehicle, please.

Wow! There is a lot to remember.

We stress important words (main verbs, nouns, adverbs, etc.) more than less important words (articles, auxiliary verbs, prepositions, pronouns, etc.).

Practice Pronunciation!

A Write the sentences in the correct columns. Then listen to check your answers.

| Close the window. | Come to see me. | What did you say? |
| What's the time? | Nice to meet you. | Where did she go? |

●･●	●･･●	●･●･

B Practice saying the sentences in **A** with your partner. Pay attention to sentence stress.

i Read

A Read the article about driving in a foreign country. What is the writer's opinion about driving in Russia?

Driving in Russia

Driving in a foreign country is always challenging. In Russia, it can be positively dangerous.

Severe weather conditions mean that roads are often hazardous outside the summer months. To make matters worse, roads outside major cities are often small and poorly maintained. Many roads in the countryside are single-lane only, meaning that cars frequently meet head-on.

People's driving habits don't help the situation. Many people drive over the speed limit, and some do not always stop at red lights.

Traffic congestion is also a major problem in cities such as Moscow and St Petersburg. In urban centers, where public transportation is usually very good, you are better off taking the subway rather than driving. That way, you can arrive on time, and in safety.

B Discuss the questions with your partner.
1. How does driving in Russia compare to driving in your country?
2. Would you drive in Russia? Why / Why not?
3. Have you ever driven in a foreign country? Tell the class about your experience.

i Write

Imagine that you are a tourist on vacation in your country. You have hired a car and spent time driving around. Write an e-mail to a friend about your experiences of driving in your country.

Lesson 4
What's your major?

Warm-Up

A Match the majors with the degrees.

Bachelor of Arts (BA)	Bachelor of Science (BS)

mathematics   English   physics   biology
TESOL   astronomy   political science   religious education
fine arts   computer programming   African studies   civil engineering
visual and performing arts   psychology   economics   sociology
statistics   music

B What are the five most popular college majors in your country?

Dialogue 1 — Listen to the dialogue and practice.

Emily: Hello, look who's here! George Mason! What are you doing here? I thought you went to California.
George: Hi, Emily! I've been hoping to see you here. I got accepted by UCLA, but I received a scholarship from Arizona.
Emily: Great! That's why I chose this college, too. Otherwise, as an out-of-state student, I couldn't afford the tuition. So, what are you studying?
George: I'm studying chemistry. I'm thinking of going to medical school later on. How about you?
Emily: Well, I chose applied linguistics as my major. I'd love to teach English and other languages as a second language.
George: That sounds good. You speak English and Vietnamese. You'll make a great ESL teacher.
Emily: Thank you. I'm sure you will be a fine doctor, too.

Comprehension Check!
1. Where are Emily and George?
2. Why did they choose to go to college in Arizona?

Language Focus

Talking about Studies	
What are you studying?	**I am studying** economics.
What's your major?	**My major's** sociology.
	I chose statistics **as my major**.
	I am an anthropology **major**.
What do you major in?	**I major in** electrical engineering.
	I major in nursing.

Talk 1

A Discuss the questions with your partner.

1. Do you think college education is important? Why / Why not?
2. If you could go back to college again, which college would you attend? What would you major in? Why?

B Read the following rules for selecting the right college. Check (✓) your answer.

	Rules for Selecting the Right College	Agree	Disagree
①	Visit colleges before making your final selection.		
②	Do some research on a few colleges that you know nothing about. You might make a good discovery.		
③	Pick three tiers of schools: reach (high), regular (middle), safety (low) schools.		
④	Discuss with your family and your counsellor.		
⑤	Check out the environment of the schools.		
⑥	Choose colleges that you are familiar with.		
⑦	Name-brand colleges guarantee your success.		
⑧	Consider the cost.		
⑨	Rely on news magazine rankings.		
⑩	Find a location that suits your personality.		

Pronunciation

Consonant Clusters

Discover Pronunciation!

Consonant clusters are groups of consonants that appear together in words.

Beginning Consonant Clusters

bl-	br-	cl-	cr-	dr-	fl-	fr-	gl-	gr-	pl-	pr-
sc-	sk-	sl-	sm-	sn-	sp-	squ-	st-	str-	sw-	tr-

Final Consonant Clusters

-ct	-ft	-lb, -lt	-mp	-nd	-ng
-nk	-nt	-pt	-sk	-sp	-st

Rare Clusters

shr- (shrink)	sph- (sphere)	thw- (thwart)

Practice Pronunciation!

A Listen to the words and practice saying them.

blame	brain	clap	crab	dress
flood	frog	glad	grab	plan
prop	scan	skin	slim	smog
snap	span	square	stop	street
swim	trip	twin	-	-

B Listen to the words and practice saying them.

blood pressure	crazy act	snowstorm
clean square	strange gift	established fact
slow jump	fly sky	clear throat

Dialogue 2 — Listen to the dialogue and practice.

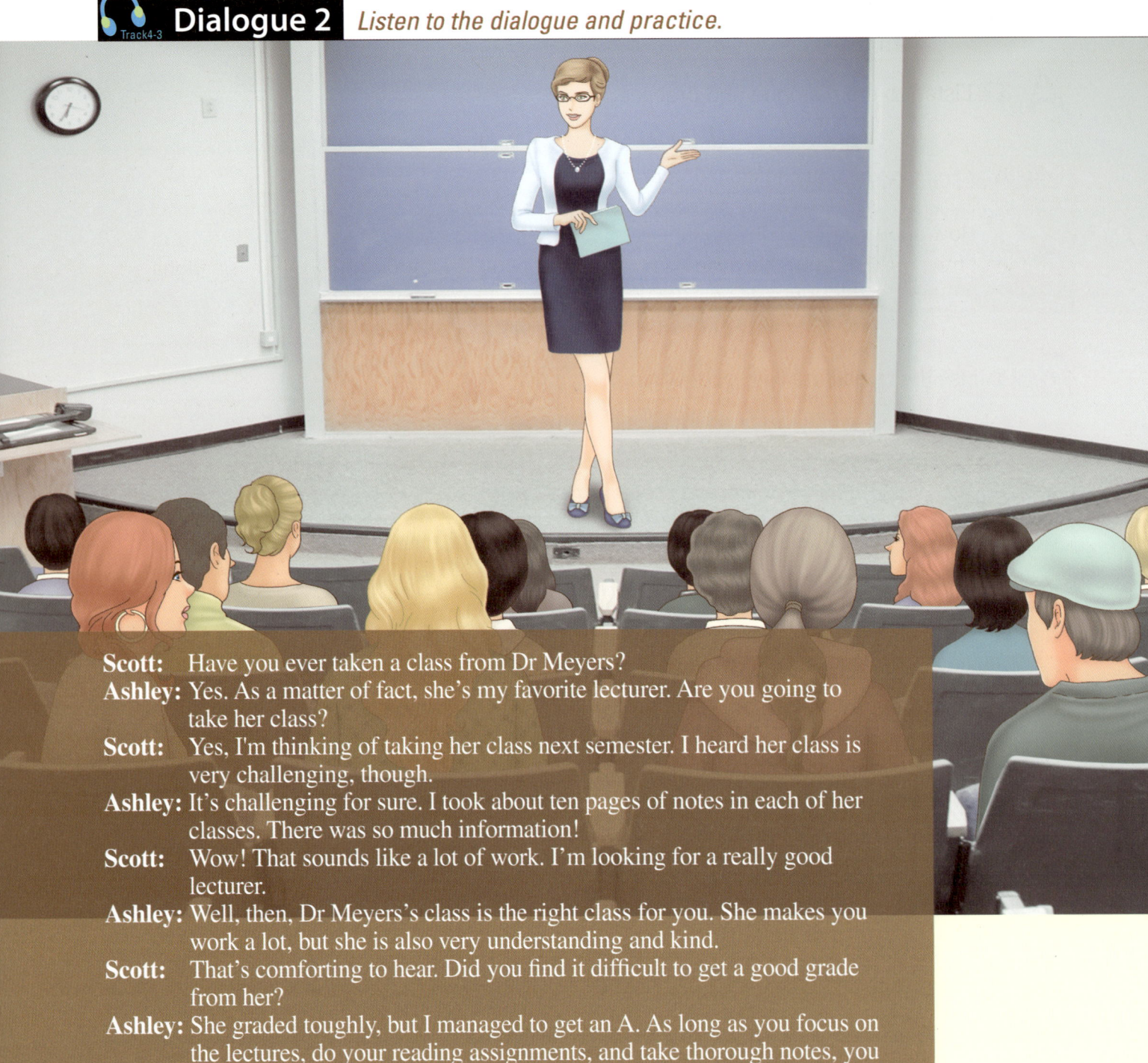

Scott: Have you ever taken a class from Dr Meyers?
Ashley: Yes. As a matter of fact, she's my favorite lecturer. Are you going to take her class?
Scott: Yes, I'm thinking of taking her class next semester. I heard her class is very challenging, though.
Ashley: It's challenging for sure. I took about ten pages of notes in each of her classes. There was so much information!
Scott: Wow! That sounds like a lot of work. I'm looking for a really good lecturer.
Ashley: Well, then, Dr Meyers's class is the right class for you. She makes you work a lot, but she is also very understanding and kind.
Scott: That's comforting to hear. Did you find it difficult to get a good grade from her?
Ashley: She graded toughly, but I managed to get an A. As long as you focus on the lectures, do your reading assignments, and take thorough notes, you will be just fine.
Scott: Great. Thanks for your advice. I'm going to sign up for her class tomorrow.
Ashley: OK. Good luck! Enjoy your class!

Comprehension Check!

1. Are Dr Meyers's classes easy?
2. Do Dr Meyers's classes require lots of note taking?

 Talk 2

A Listen to the dialogue and practice.

Emily: Ken, why did you choose to major in history?
Ken: Because I really enjoy learning about the past. I want to be a high school history teacher. How about you?
Emily: I majored in English because I wanted to be a good communicator. English is a global language, so I thought it was the best choice.

B Discuss the questions with your partner.
❶ What does Ken major in?
❷ Why did Emily choose English?

Talk 3

Read and match descriptions 1–4 with the majors in the box.

| criminal justice | history | biology | psychology |

- **Major 1:** _____
  I majored in this subject because I was interested in the study of human behaviour and the human mind. It helped me understand people better, including myself.

- **Major 2:** _____
  I chose this as my major because I planned on going to medical school. Also, I love nature and living things.

- **Major 3:** _____
  My major deals with how to investigate, prevent, and educate people about crimes. I want to work at the Department of Justice.

- **Major 4:** _____
  It is a subject that deals with significant events in the past and the explanation of their causes. It requires memorization of places, figures, and dates.

 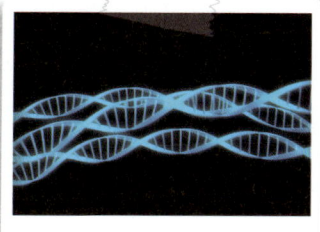  

i Read

A Read the interview with a psychologist. What does Dr Dale like about his job?

Interview with a Psychologist

Interviewer: Dr Dale, why did you choose a career in psychology?

Dr Dale: I grew up with some children in my neighborhood who were not doing well academically or socially. I wanted to help people like them.

Interviewer: What do you enjoy most about being a psychologist?

Dr Dale: I enjoy working with people, especially children. I listen to them and try to sort out their problems. I help them as much as I can. It makes me feel really good.

Interviewer: What qualities are required to be a good psychologist?

Dr Dale: You need to be a good listener. You also need to be caring and organized.

Interviewer: What different jobs are there in the field of psychology?

Dr Dale: There are a lot: psychologist, researcher, psychology teacher in high schools or colleges, therapist, and so on.

Interviewer: What are the educational requirements to become a psychologist?

Dr Dale: To work as a clinical or counseling psychologist, you must have a doctoral degree. A specialist degree in school psychology is often required to work as a school psychologist.

B Discuss the questions with your partner.
1. Why did Dr Dale choose to become a psychologist?
2. What jobs can you get if you major in psychology?

i Write

Imagine that you are having an interview. Complete the interview, using your own ideas.

Interviewer:	Why did you choose a career in _____ (*your major*)?
You:	
Interviewer:	What do you enjoy most about being a _____ (*your job*)?
You:	
Interviewer:	What qualities are required to be a good _____ (*your job*)?
You:	
Interviewer:	What different jobs are there in the field of _____ (*your major*)?
You:	
Interviewer:	What are the educational requirements to become a _____ (*your job*)?
You:	

Lesson 5
Do you want to live alone, or in a shared apartment?

Warm-Up

A Match the homes with the pictures.

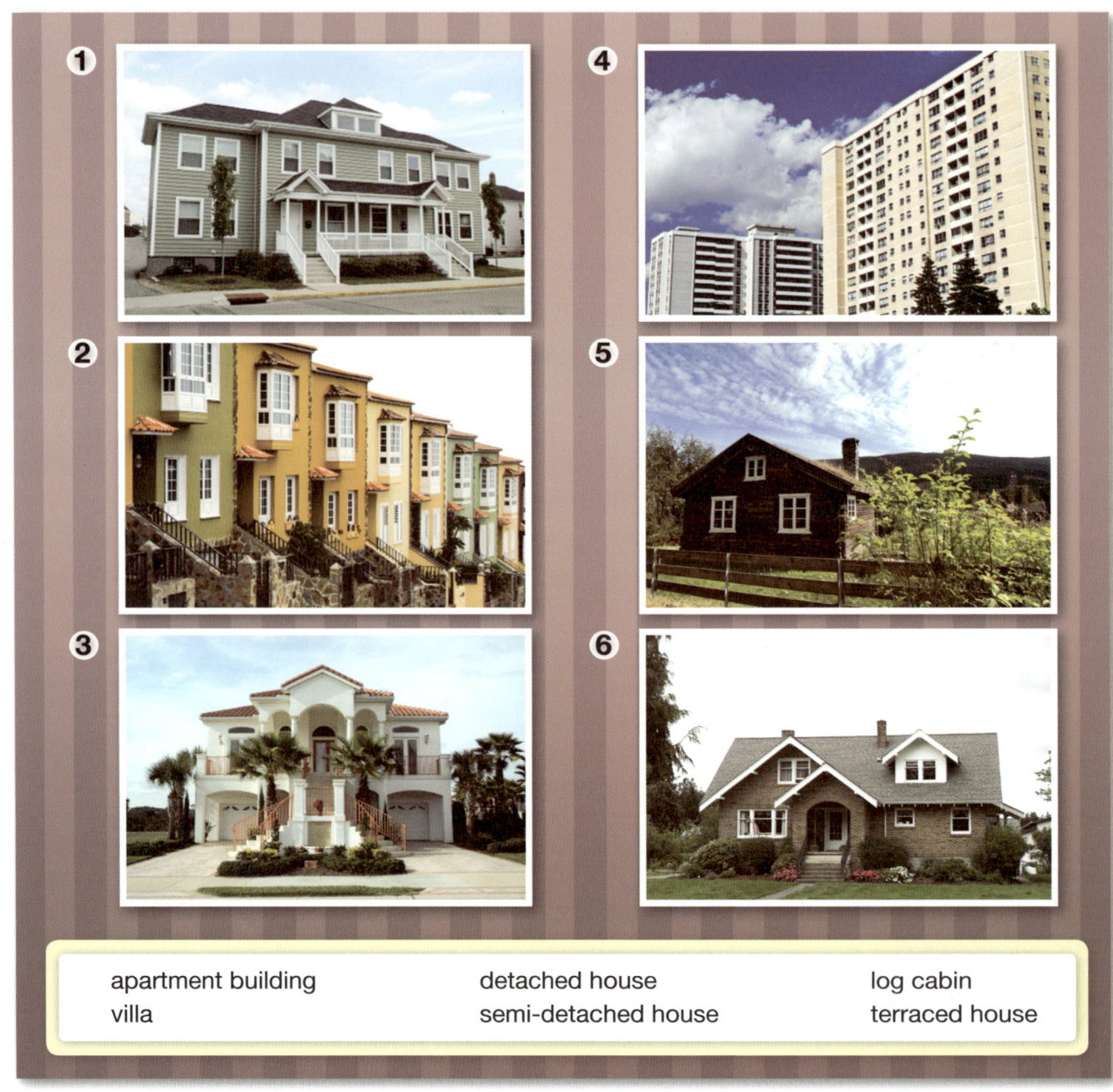

| apartment building | detached house | log cabin |
| villa | semi-detached house | terraced house |

B Discuss the questions with your partner.

1. Which of the homes in **A** is most similar to your home?
2. Which home would you most like to live in? Why?

Dialogue 1 — *Listen to the dialogue and practice.*

Letting agent:	So, how can I help you?
Jessica:	I'm starting university here in September, so I'm looking for a place to live.
Letting agent:	OK. Would you prefer a house, an apartment, or a student dormitory?
Jessica:	I'd like an apartment.
Letting agent:	I see. And, do you want to live alone, or in a shared apartment with a roommate?
Jessica:	I think I'd prefer to live alone.
Letting agent:	And what's most important to you: cost, location, or size?
Jessica:	For me, location is the most important factor. I want to be close to the university.
Letting agent:	I thought you would. We have a couple of one-bedroom apartments available in that area. The rent on both of them is 800 dollars a month. Would you like to take a look at them?
Jessica:	Yes, please.

Comprehension Check!

① What kind of home does Jessica want?

② What location does she want to live in?

Language Focus 1

Talking with Letting Agents	
How can I help you?	I'm starting university here in September, so **I'm looking for a place to live.**
Would you prefer a house, an apartment, or a student dormitory?	I'd like a house / an apartment / a student dormitory.
Do you want to live alone, or in shared accommodation with a roommate?	I'd prefer to live alone / with a roommate.
What's most important to you: cost, location, or size?	For me, location/cost/size is the most important factor.

Talk 1

 Ask three classmates questions to complete the survey.

	Classmate 1	Classmate 2	Classmate 3
❶ Kind of home preferred (house, apartment, or student dormitory)			
❷ Single or shared accommodation			
❸ Most important factor (location, size, or cost) *Give further details.*			

 Tell the class what you found out about your classmates.

Example
I found out that John wants to live alone in an apartment. For him, the most important factor is cost, because he doesn't like spending money.

Dialogue 2 — Listen to the dialogue and practice.

Judith: I was talking with my boss today. He said that within the next two years, I may have to go work overseas.
Rupert: Oh, really? Where will you go?
Judith: Well, I think I will have a choice between the London office and the Madrid office.
Rupert: Wow! I'd love to live in either of those cities. Which will you choose?
Judith: Well, I'm not sure. London may be better. I don't like hot weather, and Madrid is much hotter than London.
Rupert: Yes, but don't forget that it rains a lot more in London. Do you like rain?
Judith: No, of course I don't! I think London is a busier city than Madrid though. I like busy places.
Rupert: That may be true. But I heard that London is very expensive. Madrid is probably cheaper.
Judith: Good point. This won't be an easy decision at all!

Comprehension Check!

1. Which two cities are the speakers discussing?
2. What do the speakers say about each city?

Language Focus 2

Comparing Cities

London **may be better**.
I don't like hot weather, and Madrid **is much hotter than** London.
It rains a lot more in London.
I think London **is a busier city than** Madrid though.
I heard that London **is very expensive**. Madrid **is probably cheaper**.

Pronunciation

Sentence Stress: Unstressed Words

Discover Pronunciation!
Listen to the sentences. Notice how the speaker stresses some words more than other words.

●	•	●
Location	or	size? [conjunction]
Open	the	window. [article]
What's	your	name? [pronoun]
Go	to	sleep! [preposition]
I	can	help. [can]
She	was	late. [be]

We don't usually stress conjunctions, articles, pronouns, prepositions, or the verbs *can* and *be*.

Practice Pronunciation!

A Write the stress pattern for each sentence.

1. Close the door. ●•●
2. Where is John? ☐
3. I want a house or an apartment. ☐
4. How can I help you? ☐
5. Give it to your teacher. ☐

B Practice saying the sentences in **A** with your partner. Pay attention to sentence stress.

Talk 2

Discuss the question with your partner. Refer to the information about Hong Kong and Toronto.

Which city would be best for someone who …
- enjoys winter sports?
- hates wet weather?
- needs to find a job quickly?
- likes busy places?
- wants to buy a first home?
- likes cool weather?

Example

A: Which city would be best for someone who enjoys winter sports?
B: Well, it snows a lot in Toronto, but in Hong Kong it never snows. So, Toronto would be better.

continue

	Hong Kong	Toronto
Population	7,061,200	2,503,281
Average High Temperature °C (°F)	25.6 (78.1)	13.5 (56.3)
Average Low Temperature °C (°F)	21.1 (70)	6.0 (42.8)
Average Rainy Days	139	113
Average Snowy Days	0	42
Unemployment Rate	5.3%	9.9%
Average House Price	US$ 330,000	US$ 442,000

Talk 3

A Discuss the questions with your partner.
1. What is your favorite city to visit in the world? Why?
2. Which city in the world would you most like to live in? Why?

B Discuss with your partner which city in your country is the best for each factor.

Factor	City
good shopping	
close to nature	
exciting nightlife	
low unemployment rate	
pleasant climate	
cheap housing	
best education	
low crime rate	
clean air	
beautiful scenery	

i Read

A Read the news article. According to the article, which city is the best to live in?

World's Best City Revealed

A survey by lifestyle magazine *Monocle* has revealed the world's best cities to live in. According to the magazine's 'Most Liveable Cities Index', the best city to live in is Munich, Germany. The Index, which is compiled every year, compares cities according to a number of factors, such as safety, climate, architecture, public transportation, and health care. European cities were the biggest winners in the survey, accounting for four of the top five cities.

Top Five Best Cities
1 Munich
2 Copenhagen
3 Zurich
4 Tokyo
5 Helsinki

B Discuss the questions with your partner.

1. What factors were used in the survey to compare cities?
2. Do you agree with the factors used to compare cities? Can you think of any other important factors?
3. How well would your city perform according to the factors?

i Write

A Compare your city with another city using the factors. Make notes.

Factor	My City	Another City: _____
safety		
climate		
architecture		
public transportation		
health care		
another factor: _____		

B Write a short paragraph to compare your city with another city, using the information in **A**.

Lesson 5 · 49

Lesson 6 — That's quite a personal question.

Warm-Up

A Check (✓) whether each question is considered rude in your country.

Rude Questions?

Topic	Example Question	Yes	No	Comments
Age	How old are you?	✓		a rude question for women
Marital Status	Are you single/married/divorced?			
Relationship	Why did you break up?			
Weight	How much do you weigh?			
Income	What's your salary?			
Personal Appearance	Have you had plastic surgery / liposuction?			
Occupation	What's your occupation?			
Education	Which college did you go to?			

B Match the responses with the personal questions.

Question	Responses
How old are you?	
How much do you weigh?	
What's your salary?	

I'm old enough.   I do OK.   I earn enough to get by.
Age means nothing to me.   No comment.   Why do you ask?
Mind your own business!

Dialogue 1 — Listen to the dialogue and practice.

Roy: Hello, I'm Roy. You must be Mia. Is this your first blind date?
Mia: Hi, Roy. Yes, it is. How about you?
Roy: Same here. So, what do you do for a living?
Mia: I'm a legal assistant at a law firm. And you?
Roy: I'm a computer programmer. I want to change jobs though. How much money do you make?
Mia: That's quite a personal question. Do you need a loan or something?
Roy: No offense. I was just curious. Anyway, I'm 28 years old. How old are you?
Mia: I'd rather not say. I'm old enough!
Roy: Actually, you look fairly young. Have you had plastic surgery?
Mia: Why? What's it to you?
Roy: Sounds like you have. Have you had liposuction, too?
Mia: That's a very rude question! Excuse me. I think I'd better get going.

Comprehension Check!

1. What personal questions does Roy ask Mia?
2. Do you agree that the questions are too personal?

Language Focus 1

Personal Questions 1	
How much money do you make?	That's quite a personal question.
How old are you?	I'd rather not say.
Have you had plastic surgery?	Why? What's it to you?
Have you had liposuction, too?	That's a very rude question!

Pronunciation

Word Stress and Prefixes/Suffixes

Discover Pronunciation!
There are some rules to follow when we say words with prefixes or suffixes.

Prefixes (added at the beginning of words)

Verbs	**Short Prefixes** dis-, un-, re-, etc.	Do not stress the prefix. (It may have secondary stress.) *repórt, discóver, refléct, uncóver*
	Longer Prefixes inter-, intro-, over-, under-, fore-, etc.	Stress the verb or the root. The prefix has secondary stress. *introdúce, foretéll, oversée, undertáke*
Nouns	**Prefixes** inter-, intro-, over-, tele-, fore-, etc.	Stress the prefix. *an ínterchange, fórehead, télevision*

Suffixes (added to the end of words)

-eer, -ese, -ique, -ee	Primary stress **usually** falls on these suffixes *Japanése, employée, uníque, voluntéer*
-ial, -ual, -ian, -ion, -ious, -logy	Primary stress falls on the syllable in front of these suffixes *musícian, anthropólogy, inféction, spécial*
-ize, -ary, -ate, -ory	Primary stress falls two syllables before these suffixes *drámatize, términate, sécondary, dórmitory*
Other Suffixes	When suffixes are added to words, they usually keep the same stress as the word. wash + able = **wáshable** manage + er = **mánager** delight + ful = **delíghtful** happy + ness = **háppiness**

Practice Pronunciation!
Listen to the words and practice saying them.

❶	re-	report	react	revise	restate
❷	dis-	dismiss	disconnect	disrespect	disarray
❸	inter-	interact	intercept	interchange	international
❹	-ee	employee	refugee	nominee	referee
❺	-ion	cancellation	infection	creation	imagination
❻	-ise, -ize	exercise	emphasize	criticize	realize
❼	Other Suffixes	natural	officially	contentment	agreeable

Talk 1

Discuss the questions with your partner. Then choose your answer.

❶ What is the mood of the conversation in **Dialogue 1**?
  ⓐ pleasant　　ⓑ annoying　　ⓒ depressing　　ⓓ romantic

❷ What kind of person do you think Roy from **Dialogue 1** is?
  ⓐ considerate　　ⓑ kind　　ⓒ rude　　ⓓ boring

❸ How would you handle someone like him?
  ⓐ Tell him off.　　　　　　　　　ⓒ Knock him to the floor.
  ⓑ Report him to the police.　　ⓓ Just ignore him.

Dialogue 2 — Listen to the dialogue and practice.

Mr Jones: Come on in, Ms Evans. Have a seat.
Ms Evans: Thank you. It's nice to meet you, Mr Jones.
Mr Jones: Likewise. I saw you talking to Larry Parker just now. Do you know him?
Ms Evans: Yes, I do. Actually, he suggested I apply to this company.
Mr Jones: Really? Is he your boyfriend? You two seemed close.
Ms Evans: That's a bit personal, isn't it? If you don't mind, I'd rather not answer that question.
Mr Jones: All right. It's none of my business, I suppose. Are you available on weekends?
Ms Evans: Well, I prefer not to work on weekends. I need my own time.
Mr Jones: Are you married?
Ms Evans: That question makes me feel uncomfortable. Could you ask me job-related questions, please?

Comprehension Check!

1. Why did Ms Evans apply for a job at the company?
2. Do you think any of Mr Jones's questions are acceptable in a job interview?

Language Focus 2

Personal Questions 2	
Is he your boyfriend?	That's a bit personal, isn't it?
	If you don't mind, I'd rather not answer that question.
Are you married?	That question makes me feel uncomfortable.

Talk 2

🎧 Listen to the dialogue and practice.

Situation 1
A: Do you mind if I ask you a personal question?
B: Go ahead.
A: How much are you paid?
B: Half what I'm worth.

Situation 2
A: This might be a bit personal, but I hear you're single.
B: Oh, yeah? When did that happen?

Situation 3
A: I know it's none of my business, but how much did that cost?
B: I got a good deal. It wasn't as much as you'd think.

Talk 3

🎧 Listen to the dialogue and practice.

A: Why do people ask rude questions? They should know better.
B: You don't have to answer personal questions. Just go about your business.
A: Usually I do. But sometimes they don't give up. It's really annoying.
B: Then tell them it's none of their business.

i Read

A Read the internet article. What tips does the writer give for dealing with nosy people?

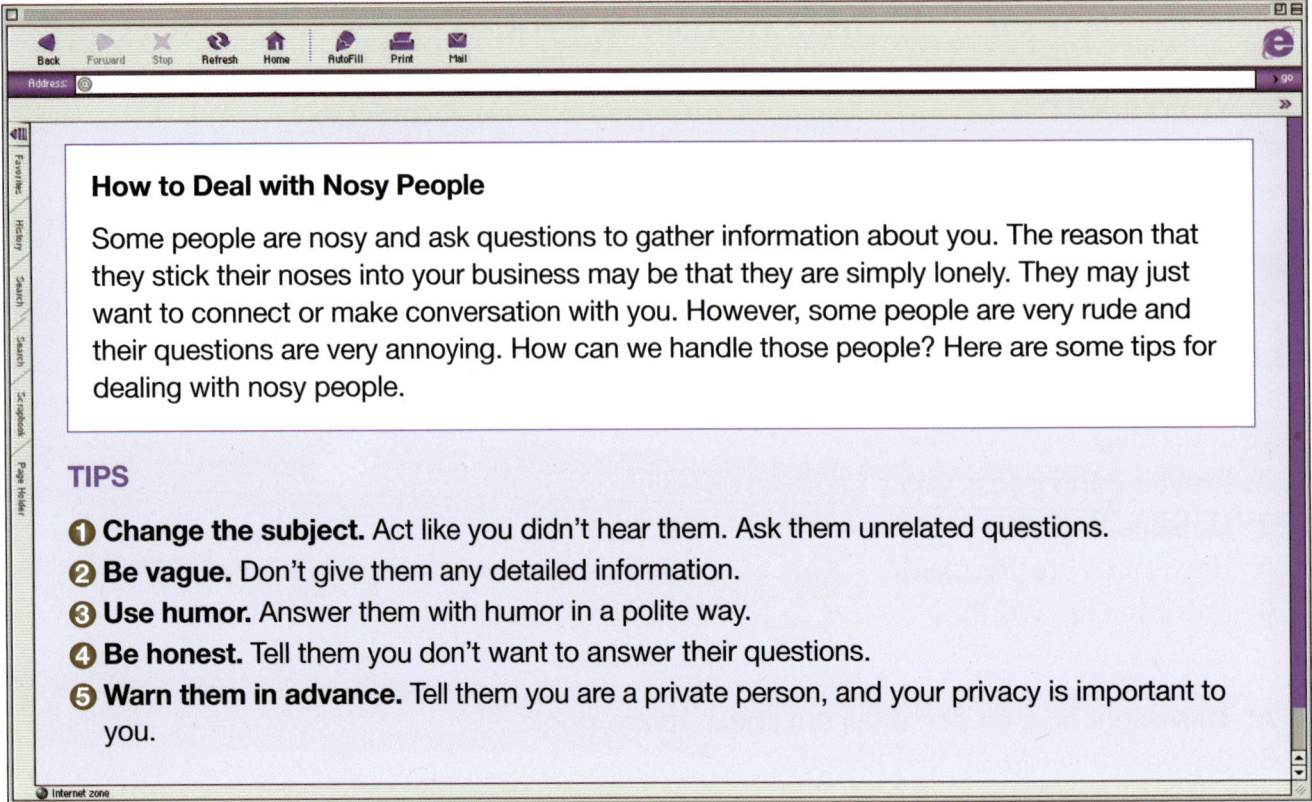

How to Deal with Nosy People

Some people are nosy and ask questions to gather information about you. The reason that they stick their noses into your business may be that they are simply lonely. They may just want to connect or make conversation with you. However, some people are very rude and their questions are very annoying. How can we handle those people? Here are some tips for dealing with nosy people.

TIPS

1. **Change the subject.** Act like you didn't hear them. Ask them unrelated questions.
2. **Be vague.** Don't give them any detailed information.
3. **Use humor.** Answer them with humor in a polite way.
4. **Be honest.** Tell them you don't want to answer their questions.
5. **Warn them in advance.** Tell them you are a private person, and your privacy is important to you.

B Match tips 1–5 in **A** with the responses.

Question	Response	Tip Number
How much do you make?	I earn enough to get by.	2
I hear you're single.	Oh, yeah? When did that happen?	
Are you married?	That question makes me feel uncomfortable.	
How much do you weigh?	I'm thirsty. Can I get you something to drink?	
Do you mind if I ask you a personal question?	Yes, I do. I'm a private person.	

i Write

Write an answer for each question, referring to the tips in *i* **Read**.

Question	Response
❶ How old are you?	
❷ Are you married?	
❸ Do you have children?	
❹ Do you live alone?	
❺ Do you have a boyfriend/girlfriend?	
❻ How much do you weigh?	
❼ Are you on a diet?	
❽ How much money do you make?	
❾ What's your phone number?	
❿ How much did you pay for that?	

Lesson 7 — What kind of treatment did you get?

Warm-Up

A Match the treatments with the pictures.

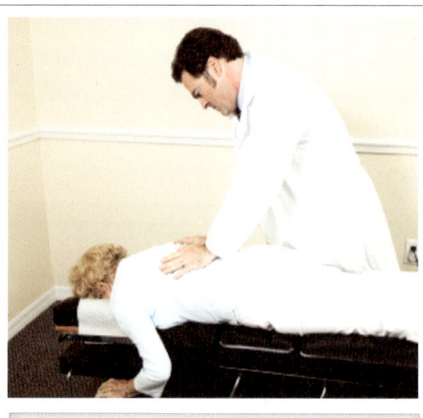

| massage | chiropractic adjustment | acupuncture |
| cupping therapy | herbal medicine | enzyme bath |

B Which of the treatments in **A** have you tried? Did you like them?

Dialogue 1
Listen to the dialogue and practice.

Kate: Hi, Ron. What's the matter? You don't look well.
Ron: Hello, Kate. My shoulder and neck are killing me! They hurt so much, I can't do anything.
Kate: I know what you mean. I've had the same problem before. I had to get some treatment.
Ron: What kind of treatment did you get?
Kate: Well, I had a chiropractic adjustment. The doctor adjusted my spine and joints. After that, I felt much better.
Ron: Really? Did you hear a cracking sound during the treatment? I saw it on TV, and it scared me!
Kate: Oh, yes. I was very nervous at first. But once you get used to it, you learn to relax.
Ron: Maybe I should try it. Could you give me the doctor's phone number?
Kate: Sure, I'll give it to you now. The sooner you take care of it, the better.
Ron: Thank you so much, Kate. I'll treat you to lunch sometime!

Comprehension Check!

1. What is the matter with Ron?
2. What did Kate do when she had Ron's problem?

Language Focus 1

Talking about Health 1

What's the matter?	My shoulder and neck are killing me!
	My feet are killing me!
	My back is killing me!
What kind of treatment did you get?	I got chiropractic treatment.
	I got a massage.
	I got cupping therapy.

Talk 1

Discuss the questions with your partner.

1. When you have pain in your shoulder or back, what do you do?
   - a. go see a doctor
   - b. get a massage
   - c. use a hot pack
   - d. take a pain reliever

2. Do you think alternative treatments, such as acupuncture and herbal medicines, work?
   - a. Yes. They work because _____.
   - b. No. They don't work because _____.

Pronunciation

Thought Groups and Intonation

Discover Pronunciation!
Thought groups are phrases that express separate ideas. Thought groups help listeners understand the meaning of a sentence.

Thought Groups and Grammatical Phrases
Grammatical phrases are often used as thought groups.

Prepositional Phrases	at the airport, at noon, in the classroom
Short Clauses	When you get there, call me. If you are thirsty, you can have some ice tea.
Verb + Pronoun/Noun	go swimming, get it, go home
Determiner + Noun	your dog, my phone, the car

Joining Thought Groups Together
We pause briefly after the last word in a thought group.

My friends ⇧ came over to the club house ⇧ for our science project.
       pause   pause

Thought Groups and Intonation
There is usually a small rise or fall at the end of a thought group.

My train ↗ is leaving ↗ at 9 o'clock. ↘

If you don't want to be late, ↗ we should start now. ↘

Practice Pronunciation!
Listen to the sentences and practice saying them.

1. She finished her English report.
2. I don't understand why they didn't support the President.
3. My sister and I went swimming at the community center yesterday.
4. Could you give me your dentist's phone number?
5. Boil some water and add some ginger root.

Dialogue 2
Listen to the dialogue and practice.

Marie: Here you go, Kenny. I've fixed you some ginger tea.
Kenny: Ginger tea? Thank you. But why? What's it for?
Marie: It's for your cold. You've been coughing a lot. Ginger is especially good for colds and sore throats.
Kenny: I didn't know that. Let me have a taste. [pause] Yes, it's pretty good. How do you make it?
Marie: You boil some water and then add some ginger root. Let it simmer for about 15 to 20 minutes. Then add honey and lemon, if you want.
Kenny: That's pretty simple. People use so many different methods to stay healthy, don't they?
Marie: Yes, you're right. There's both modern and alternative medicine. When I have a headache, I get acupressure treatment instead of taking pills.
Kenny: That sounds interesting. Does it really work?
Marie: Yes, it does. It also has no side effects. You should give it a try.

Comprehension Check!

1. Why did Marie make ginger tea?
2. Besides drinking ginger tea, what other treatments are mentioned in the dialogue?

Language Focus 2

Talking about Health 2

I have fixed some ginger tea for you.
I have fixed dinner for you.
You've been cough**ing** a lot.
You've been sneez**ing** a lot.
That sounds interesting.
That sounds incredible!

 ## Talk 2

🎧 Listen to the dialogue and practice.

A: Besides taking medication, what do you do if you have a stomachache?
B: I drink peppermint tea. It really works.

A: Besides taking medication, what do you do if you have a cold?
B: I eat chicken soup and rest. That's the best remedy for me.

A: I'm so tired. What do you suggest?
B: Why don't you get a massage? That would be relaxing.

Talk 3

A Complete the table, giving your suggestions for each symptom.

Symptom	Modern Medicine	Alternative Medicine
sore throat	penicillin	
backache		massage
headache		acupressure
fever	aspirin	

B Practice asking and answering the questions with your partner. Refer to the table in **A**.

A: What do you do to treat a sore throat?
B: _____.

A: What do you do if you have backache?
B: _____.

A: Besides taking medication, what can you do to reduce a fever?
B: _____.

i Read

A Read the posts from an internet health forum.

Seeking Acupuncturist Recommendations
JD from Phoenix, Arizona, on June 21

> Hello! I'm new to Phoenix and looking for a good acupuncturist. I've been receiving acupuncture treatment for lower back pain for several months. If you could recommend someone, I would appreciate it. Thanks!

Responses

> Hi, I recommend Dr Johnny Wang. He is really good and experienced. His phone number is 480-556-1324.
> Chris

> Hello! Contact Super Nature Clinic at 602-555-0487. They have many friendly acupuncturists with good reputations.
> Debbie

B Discuss the questions with your partner.
1. Why is JD looking for an acupuncturist?
2. If you were JD, which would you choose: Dr Wang or Super Nature Clinic? Why?

i Write

Write a reply to JD in *i* **Read** to recommend a different treatment for his/her back pain.

Lesson 8 What is an American wedding like?

Warm-Up

A Match the countries with the pictures of wedding ceremonies.

Country: _____	Country: _____
Country: _____	Country: _____
Country: _____	Country: _____

Korea   Greece   Nigeria   India   England   Japan

B Talk with your partner about wedding traditions in your country. What do the bride and groom wear? What is the wedding reception like?

Dialogue 1 *Listen to the dialogue and practice.*

Michelle: Wow, are these your wedding pictures? You look so beautiful!
Su-mi: Thank you. Our photographer captured our wedding perfectly.
Michelle: You are wearing different wedding dresses in the pictures. Did you have two wedding ceremonies?
Su-mi: No, we didn't. Nowadays many Korean weddings are a mixture of western and traditional styles. The bride and groom wear western clothes for the first part of the ceremony. Then, they change into traditional clothes for the second part.
Michelle: Traditional Korean clothes are so gorgeous! What did you do during the traditional part of the ceremony?
Su-mi: We took part in a custom called *pyebaek*. It's attended by family members only. During *pyebaek*, the bride formally greets her new parents-in-law.
Michelle: How interesting! In my country, the couple usually goes to a reception right after the ceremony. People give toasts to the couple and wish them happiness.
Su-mi: Would you like to attend a traditional Korean wedding ceremony? If you want, I'll take you to one.
Michelle: Really? That sounds terrific! It'll help me understand Korean culture much better.

Comprehension Check!

① What happens at a Korean wedding ceremony?
② What are Michelle and Su-mi going to do together?

Language Focus 1

Weddings 1

Would you like to attend a **traditional wedding ceremony**?
We had our **wedding pictures** taken before the ceremony.
Western **wedding dresses** are usually white.
People give toasts to the couple at the **reception**.

Talk 1

Discuss the questions with your partner and complete the table.

1. What kind of clothes do you want to wear at your modern/traditional wedding?
2. Where will the ceremony be held?
3. What kind of transportation will you use to get to the wedding venue?
4. Who will perform the wedding ceremony?

Modern Wedding	Traditional Wedding
•	•
•	•
•	•
•	•

Pronunciation

Rhythm Patterns

Discover Pronunciation!

Prepositions (Unstressed)
Short prepositions in prepositional phrases are not stressed.
*at **níght**, at **schóol**, for an **hóur***

Of
We usually pronounce *of* as /əv/. However, we sometimes pronounce it as /ə/ and we link the sound with surrounding sounds.
a cup of coffee → *a /**cuppə**/ coffee*
a couple of friends → *a /**coupələ**/ friends*

Separated Two-Word Verbs
We stress prepositions when they are part of a separated two-word verb.
*try them **ón**, finish it **óff**, look it **úp***

Practice Pronunciation!
Listen to the words and practice saying them.

1. bring them **back**
2. leave it **alone**
3. put the pictures **away**
4. fill it **out**
5. wake us **up**
6. turn the volume **down**
7. by **bus**
8. on **time**
9. at **home**
10. a **couple of** minutes
11. a **cup of** coffee
12. a **ton of** food

Dialogue 2
Listen to the dialogue and practice.

Akiko: Hello, Ryan! I hear your sister's getting married.
Ryan: Hi, Akiko. Yes, she's getting married in six weeks. She's going to send the wedding invitations soon. She'll send you one, too.
Akiko: I'll be happy to attend her wedding. What is an American wedding like? Are there any unique traditions?
Ryan: Well, before the wedding, the maid of honor throws a bridal shower. The bride-to-be receives gifts from her female friends.
Akiko: I see. What about the groom? Does he get anything from his friends?
Ryan: Actually, the groom hosts a bachelor party right before the wedding day. He and his male friends enjoy his last moments of freedom as a single man.
Akiko: Last moments of freedom? I think that's funny! OK, what else?
Ryan: Gifts are very important. People give gifts to the couple for their new home, or they give cash.
Akiko: In Japan, we don't bring gifts, but we do give money. We also pay an entrance fee to attend the wedding party.
Ryan: Really? I didn't know that. Well, you don't have to pay for the reception at my sister's wedding. Just come and have a good time!
Akiko: I sure will! I'll be looking forward to it.

Comprehension Check!

1. What are the traditions of an American wedding?
2. How is a Japanese wedding party different from an American wedding party?

Language Focus 2

Weddings 2

I hear your sister's getting married.
I hear you're getting engaged.
I hear you're moving to LA.

What is an American wedding **like?**
What is the bride **like?**

I'll be looking forward to it.
I'll be looking forward to see**ing** you.
I'll be looking forward to hear**ing** from you.

Talk 2

 Read the interesting facts about weddings around the world.

Ancient Greece and Rome	People believed that veils could protect brides from evil spirits. Brides have worn veils ever since.
Australia	The oldest bride in Australian history was 102 years old. The groom was 82 years old.
China	A Chinese bride wore the longest wedding gown ever. It was 2,162 meters long.
Morocco	Women take a milk bath to purify themselves before their wedding ceremony.
England	Queen Victoria's wedding cake weighed nearly 300 pounds.
Israel	An Israeli wedding had the highest attendance in the world: 30,000 people.
Philippines	The best month to marry is December.

B Ask and answer the questions with your partner.

Q & A

A: How much did Queen Victoria's wedding cake weigh?
B: It weighed _____.
A: What did ancient Greeks and Romans think about veils?
B: They thought _____.
A: How long was the longest wedding gown?
B: It was _____.
A: Who takes a milk bath before their wedding ceremony?
B: _____ take a milk bath before their wedding ceremony.
A: When is the best month to marry in the Philippines?
B: The best month is _____.
A: What was the highest attendance at a wedding?
B: The highest attendance was _____.
A: How old was the oldest bride in Australia?
B: She was _____.

Talk 3

 A Match the countries with the traditional wedding foods.

1. Thailand
2. Vietnam
3. Ireland
4. Mexico
5. Italy

a. beef or chicken, warm tortillas, enchiladas, sangria
b. pasta, soup, meat, salads, confetti
c. Irish whiskey cake with mead (honey wine)
d. lots of seafood, long noodles
e. *foy thong* – a dessert made of egg yolks and sugar syrup

B Ask and answer the questions with your partner.

| What do you eat on a wedding day in Thailand? Vietnam Ireland Mexico Italy | You eat … |

i Read

A Read the wedding invitation. When and where will the wedding take place?

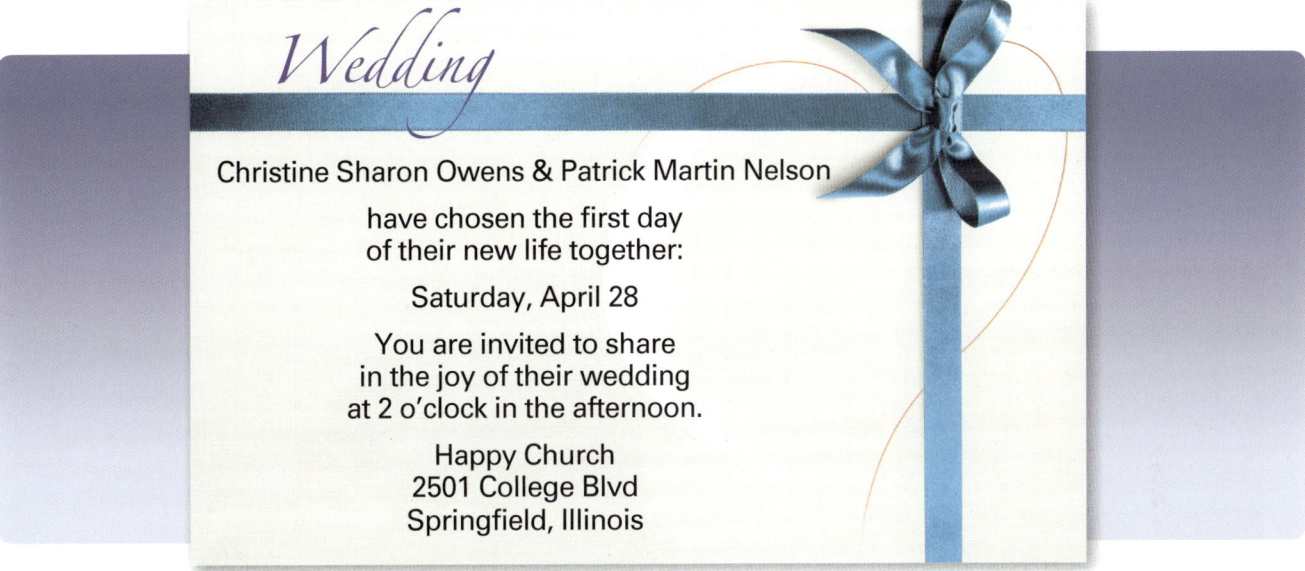

Wedding

Christine Sharon Owens & Patrick Martin Nelson

have chosen the first day
of their new life together:

Saturday, April 28

You are invited to share
in the joy of their wedding
at 2 o'clock in the afternoon.

Happy Church
2501 College Blvd
Springfield, Illinois

B Discuss the questions with your partner.
1. Who is getting married?
2. What kind of wedding ceremony do you think it will be? Why?

i Write

Complete the wedding invitation for your best friend.

Wedding

_____ & _____
(name of bride) (name of groom)

have chosen the first day
of their new life together:

_____
(date)

You are invited to share
in the joy of their wedding

at _____
(time)

Happy Church
2501 College Blvd
Springfield, Illinois

Lesson 9
I ran a red light.

Warm-Up

A Match the crimes with the pictures.

① _____
② _____
③ _____
④ _____
⑤ _____
⑥ _____

| vandalism   assault and battery   identity theft   drunk driving   arson   pick pocketing |

B Discuss the questions with your partner.
① Which crime in **A** do you think is the most serious?
② In your opinion, what should be the punishment for each crime?

Dialogue 1 — Listen to the dialogue and practice.

Steve: Guess what. I got a traffic ticket today.
Nicole: Really? What for?
Steve: For running a red light. I didn't notice that I did it. I heard a siren, and then I saw a police car flashing its lights behind me.
Nicole: So, what did you do?
Steve: I pulled over to the side of the road. The police officer got out of the car and told me I had run a red light.
Nicole: Did you tell him that you didn't know?
Steve: Yes, I did. I told him in a polite way. But he wrote me a ticket anyway.
Nicole: Couldn't he have just given you a warning? I got pulled over once, but I only got a warning.
Steve: Well, you did, but I didn't. This police officer went by the book. Now I have to go to court.
Nicole: Court? What's going to happen?
Steve: The judge will decide how much my fine will be.

Comprehension Check!

1. Why did Steve get into trouble?
2. Why does he have to go to court?

Language Focus 1

Traffic Offenses

I got a **traffic ticket** today.
I **ran a red light**.
I **got pulled over**.
He **wrote me a ticket**.
The police officer **went by the book**.

Pronunciation

/s/ and /z/

Discover Pronunciation!

/s/ is voiceless. We make a sound like a snake: Sssssssss.

/z/ is voiced. We make a sound like a bee: Zzzzzzzzzz.

	/s/		/z/
s	yes, same, this	z	zoo, zebra, lazy
ss	asset, class, possible	zz	buzz, dizzy
se	course, promise, house	ze/se	size, wise
c	center, city, nice	s	busy, choose, please
sc	scene, science, scissors	ss	scissors, dessert
x	excellent, next, Texas	x	exam, exactly

Practice Pronunciation!
Listen and write /s/ or /z/ next to each word. Then practice saying the words.

❶ crazy ☐ ❷ civil ☐ ❸ noise ☐ ❹ choice ☐
❺ kiss ☐ ❻ risen ☐ ❼ talks ☐ ❽ loose ☐
❾ reason ☐ ❿ box ☐ ⓫ works ☐ ⓬ music ☐
⓭ horse ☐ ⓮ choose ☐ ⓯ sings ☐ ⓰ easy ☐

Talk 1

A Ask your partner questions about the traffic violations.

Have you ever been pulled over? How many times?	Yes, _____. / No, _____. Just once.
Have you ever run a red light? How many times?	Yes, _____. / No, _____.
Have you ever gotten a traffic ticket? How many times?	Yes, _____. / No, _____.
Have you ever paid a fine? How many times?	Yes, _____. / No, _____.
Have you ever driven while drunk? How many times?	Yes, _____. / No, _____.
Have you ever had a car accident? How many times?	Yes, _____. / No, _____.

B Describe what has happened in each picture.

She  _____.   He _____.

He  _____.   They _____.

He  _____.   They _____.

Dialogue 2 — Listen to the dialogue and practice.

Kim: Dan, did you hear about the robbery at Central Bank?
Dan: Did I hear about it?! I was right there when it happened!
Kim: You've got to be kidding! Are you serious?
Dan: Yes, I'm serious. I was sitting on the couch waiting for my turn. All of a sudden, two men wearing masks came in. They were holding guns.
Kim: Oh my! Then what happened?
Dan: One of the guys shouted, 'Everybody get down on the floor!' People panicked and just followed his instruction.
Kim: Weren't you scared when you saw the guns?
Dan: I sure was. I tried not to look at the robbers. But I managed to remember some things about them.
Kim: Did you talk to the police about what you saw?
Dan: Yes, I did. I told them about the robbers' clothing and height, and about their weapons. I hope the police catch them soon.

Comprehension Check!

1. Where did the robbery take place?
2. How did Dan help the police?

Language Focus 2

Talking about Robbery

Did you hear about the **robbery**?
You've got to be kidding!
All of a sudden, two men wearing masks came in.
They were **holding guns**.
People **panicked** and just followed his instruction.

Talk 2

A Practice the dialogue with your partner.

Police: Jimmy Henderson, you are under arrest for bank robbery.
Jimmy: What? What are you talking about? I didn't commit a crime!
Police: You have the right to remain silent. Anything you say can and will be used against you in a court of law. You have the right to an attorney. If you cannot afford an attorney, one will be provided for you. Do you understand the rights I have just read to you?

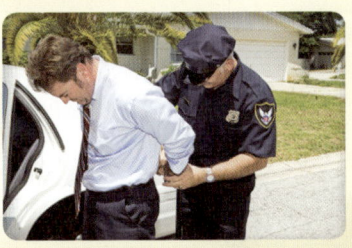

B Discuss the questions with your partner.

❶ What are the man's rights under arrest? Check (✓) the correct statements.

He can remain silent. ☐
He cannot have a lawyer if he has no money. ☐
Anything he says will be used against him in court. ☐
He must answer all questions. ☐
He can talk to the police at his own will. ☐

❷ Do you think the man will need a lawyer? Why / Why not?

 **Talk 3**

A Listen to the dialogue and practice.

Officer: May I help you?
Victim: Yes. I'd like to file a complaint. My car was stolen.
Officer: When did it happen?
Victim: Sometime between yesterday evening and this morning. I parked the car in front of my house around 8:30. When I went outside to get the newspaper this morning, it was gone!

B Discuss the questions with your partner.

1. Where is this conversation most likely taking place?
2. What is the victim doing?
3. What happened to the victim's car?
4. Where was the car parked?

Read

A Read the news stories. What is each story about?

NEWS IN BRIEF

Former Congressman Pleads Not Guilty
Former congressman Jerry Low pleaded not guilty to two corruption charges. Low is charged with two counts of bribery. His attorney said that he is looking to have all the charges dismissed.

East LA Man Pleads Guilty
An East LA man pleaded guilty to possession of illegal drugs with intent to supply. Larry Hopper, 32, has a previous felony drug conviction. Because of this record, he may receive a sentence of between ten years and life in prison.

Teenager Facing Trial on Felony Charges
An 18-year-old teenager is facing trial on felony charges of robbery and kidnapping.
Aaron Morgan pleaded not guilty to the charges this morning. He will return to court on August 16.

B Check (✓) whether each statement is true or false.

1	Jerry Low used to be a congressman.	true ☐	false ☐
2	He is accused of accepting bribes.	true ☐	false ☐
3	Larry Hopper wanted to sell illegal drugs.	true ☐	false ☐
4	His maximum prison term could be 10 years.	true ☐	false ☐
5	Aaron Morgan's charges are felonies.	true ☐	false ☐
6	He had a trial this morning.	true ☐	false ☐

i Write

Complete the sentences, using the appropriate words from the box.

Jimmy: I need your help.
Lawyer: _____?
Jimmy: _____.
Lawyer: That's a felony. _____.
Jimmy: _____.
Lawyer: _____ $200 per hour.
Jimmy: _____.
Lawyer: Sorry, but _____.
Jimmy: Well, I guess _____. OK, _____.

What can I do for you
you're hired
I'm being charged with bank robbery
that's my rate
I can help you with that
How much do you charge
I charge
I have no choice
That's pretty expensive

Lesson 10
What's your emergency?

Warm-Up

A Complete the sentences, referring to the pictures.

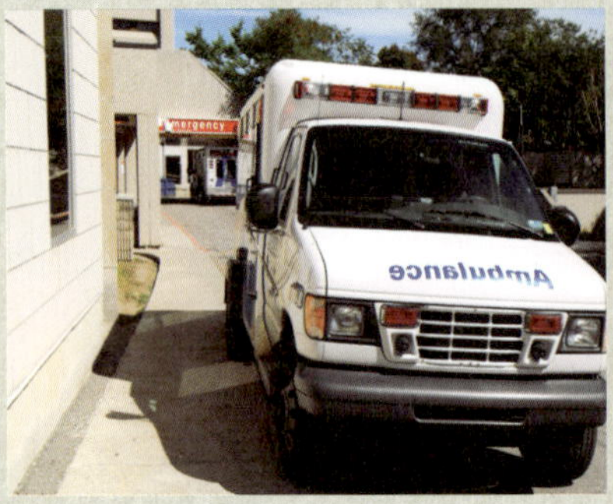

| ambulance | fire fighters | burglary |
| car accident | tsunami | chest pain |

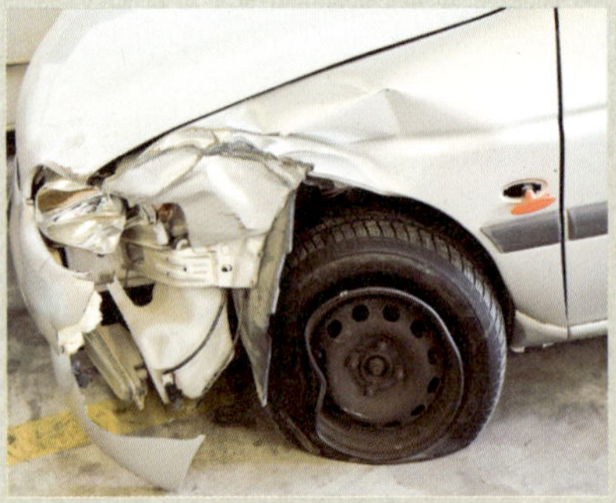

1. I'd like to report a _____. Someone is breaking into my house!
2. An _____ is a vehicle used for transporting sick or injured people.
3. A massive _____ hit Japan and caused major damage in northern areas.
4. One of the _____ was injured while attending a San Francisco house fire.
5. I was in a big _____ last year. It cost me $2,000 to fix my car.
6. Ron had severe _____ last night. His wife called 911 for help.

B Discuss the questions with your partner.
1. What is an emergency?
2. What should you do in an emergency?

Dialogue 1 — Listen to the dialogue and practice.

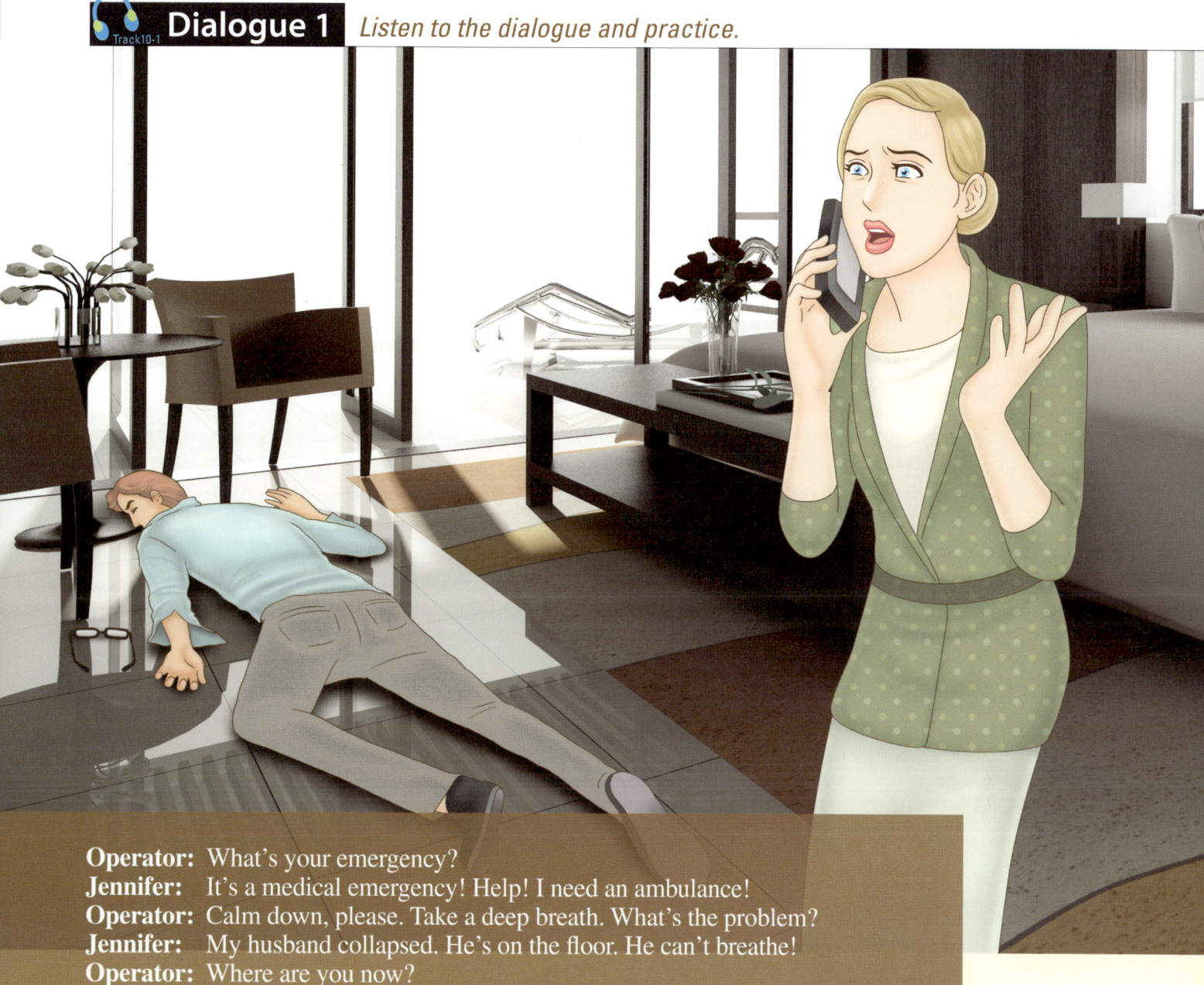

Operator: What's your emergency?
Jennifer: It's a medical emergency! Help! I need an ambulance!
Operator: Calm down, please. Take a deep breath. What's the problem?
Jennifer: My husband collapsed. He's on the floor. He can't breathe!
Operator: Where are you now?
Jennifer: We're at home. The address is 2013 75th Place, Blooming Garden.
Operator: What's your name?
Jennifer: My name's Jennifer Gomez. Please, hurry!
Operator: Is your husband still conscious?
Jennifer: Yes, he is.
Operator: Is your front door unlocked? If not, could you unlock the door, please?
Jennifer: OK. I did it.
Operator: Good. Now stay on the line. I've dispatched an ambulance. It's on the way.

Comprehension Check!

1. Why did Jennifer call the emergency number?
2. What did the operator do for Jennifer?

Language Focus 1

Emergencies 1

What's your emergency?	I need an ambulance. I'd like to report a burglary. There's been a car accident. A fire broke out in my neighborhood.

Pronunciation

Words Used as Nouns and Verbs

Discover Pronunciation!

Some words are nouns when they are stressed on the first syllable, and verbs when they are stressed on the second syllable.

Nouns		Verbs	
áddress	the place	addréss	to direct a speech
récord	a written official report	recórd	to set down in writing
défect	a shortcoming or fault	deféct	to desert one's country
présent	a gift	presént	to bring or give
súspect	a person who is suspected	suspéct	to doubt

Practice Pronunciation!

Listen to the words and practice saying them.

	Nouns	Verbs
❶	áddict	addíct
❷	rébel	rebél
❸	próduce	prodúce
❹	désert	desért
❺	pérmit	permít
❻	cónvert	convért
❼	óbject	objéct
❽	fínance	finánce
❾	ínsult	insúlt
❿	cónvict	convíct

Talk 1

Talk with your partner about emergency numbers in different countries, using the information in the chart.

Country	Police	Medical	Fire
South Korea	112	119	
Singapore	999	995	
South Africa	10111	10177	10111
Israel	100	101	102
Egypt	122	123	180
Turkey	155	112	110
Philippines	117		
United States	911		

Example

A: What's the emergency number in South Korea?
B: It's 112 for police and 119 for medical and fire.

1. **A:** What's the emergency number in South Africa?
   B: ______________________________.
2. **A:** What's the emergency number in Israel?
   B: ______________________________.
3. **A:** What's the emergency number in Turkey?
   B: ______________________________.
4. **A:** ______________________________?
   B: It's 117 for police, medical, and fire.
5. **A:** ______________________________?
   B: It's 911 for police, medical, and fire.
6. In Singapore, call __________ for police, __________ for medical, and __________ for fire.
7. In Egypt, call __________ for police, __________ for medical, and __________ for fire.

Dialogue 2
Listen to the dialogue and practice.

Pedro: Susan! Thank God you're safe! Are you OK?
Susan: Yes. I was just scared. I hope everyone got out of the building.
Pedro: I hope so, too. What happened? How did the fire start?
Susan: All of a sudden, the fire alarm went off. Then I heard people shouting 'fire' in the hallway.
Pedro: It was a close call. How did you manage to get out?
Susan: Thanks to the fire drills I practiced, I didn't panic. I got out of the apartment as quickly as possible.
Pedro: That's the most important thing. Look! There's a woman yelling out for help! She's trapped in her apartment!
Susan: There's a fire fighter climbing up the ladder. He's got her now. They're coming down together.
Pedro: Fires are so scary and dangerous. We should be careful all the time.
Susan: You're right. Prevention is the best protection.

Comprehension Check!

1. What emergency are Pedro and Susan discussing?
2. How did Susan find out about the emergency? What did she do?

Language Focus 2

Emergencies 2
I was scared/nervous/upset. She's trapped in her apartment / an elevator / a car.

Talk 2

A Complete the sentences, using the appropriate words from the boxes.

Emergency Tips

❶ Earthquake
- If you are indoors, stay inside.
- Drop, _____!
- Stay away from _____.
- If you are outdoors, _____.
- If you are in a car, _____.

| windows and doors | slow down and drive to a clear place |
| drop to the ground | cover and hold on |

❷ Car Accident
- Stay calm. Do not panic.
- Call the _____.
- Contact your _____.
- _____ admit fault.
- _____ information with the other driver in the accident.

| insurance company | never | exchange | police |

❸ Fire
- Do not _____ when escaping a fire.
- If you see smoke coming under the door, _____.
- _____ and crawl on your hands and knees under the smoke.
- If your clothes catch fire, _____!

| take an elevator | stay low to the floor | stop, drop, and roll | don't open the door |

B Talk with your partner about what to do in each of the emergencies in **A**.

> **Example**
> **A:** What should you do if there is an earthquake?
> **B:** If you are indoors, stay inside. Then, ⋯ continue

Talk 3

A 🎧 Listen to the dialogue and practice.

Clark: Hey, Janet, what happened to Joe? Why is he in the hospital?
Janet: You haven't heard about the accident, Clark?
Clark: No, I haven't. What accident?
Janet: His car flipped over on Freeway 77.
Clark: Really? How is he? Did he get hurt?
Janet: Luckily, he's doing OK. But his car was beyond the repair. It was totaled.

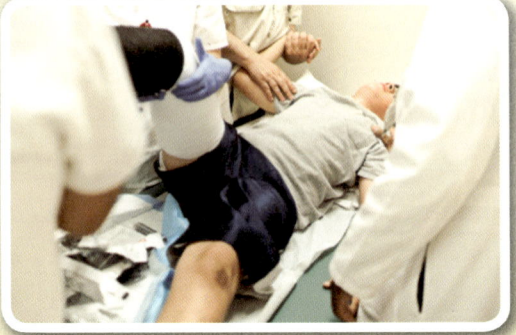

B Discuss the questions with your partner.
❶ What happened to Joe?
❷ Where did the accident happen?
❸ What happened to his car?

i Read

A Read the news stories. What is each story about?

NEWS HEADLINES

Brave Dogs Save Lives
- A family dog saved a three-month-old baby from a fire.
- An 18-week-old dog saved a boy by chasing bees away.
- A stray dog saved an abandoned newborn baby.

Emergency Landings
- An airplane made an emergency landing after an instrument malfunction.
- A small airplane exploded after an emergency landing.
- An airplane made an emergency landing in the Hudson River.

Hurricanes Hit
- A category five hurricane hit El Salvador.
- Tens of thousands of people lost their homes in New Orleans. The most devastating damage was caused by flooding.

B Check (✓) whether each question is true or false, referring to the news stories in **A**.

1	A stray dog saved a baby from a fire.	true ☐	false ☐
2	Flooding caused great damage.	true ☐	false ☐
3	A hurricane destroyed many homes in New Orleans.	true ☐	false ☐
4	A plane failed to make an emergency landing in the Hudson River.	true ☐	false ☐

i Write

Put the words in the correct order to make news headlines.

5-year-old girl	saves	in a house	Dog	rushed	his owner	Fire
calls	911 for help	broke out	Man	to the hospital with a heart attack	

1.
2.
3.
4.

Lesson 11: What kind of job are you interested in?

Warm-Up

A Match the jobs with the pictures. Then talk about what you would like and dislike about each job.

chemist   author   movie director   farmer   salesperson   accountant

B Discuss the questions with your partner.

1. What do your friends and family do for a living?
2. What do your friends and family like and dislike about their jobs?

Dialogue 1
Listen to the dialogue and practice.

Oscar: Hey, Penny. I thought I may run into you here. How's the job hunting going?
Penny: Not bad. I've talked with a few interesting employers here. How about you? What kind of job are you looking for?
Oscar: Well, I'm looking for a full-time job with good pay. I'd also like a job with a retirement plan and health insurance. That would be perfect! What kind of job are you interested in?
Penny: I want to work for a company that has good training programs. Then, when I'm older, I can go freelance using the skills I've learned. I don't want to be an office worker my whole life!
Oscar: Yes, I guess it would be nice to work freelance. That way you can be your own boss.
Penny: Exactly! Anyway, let's get on with our job hunting. See you later!
Oscar: Yes, and good luck!

Comprehension Check!

1. Where most likely are the speakers?
2. What kind of jobs do Oscar and Penny want?

Language Focus 1

Talking about Jobs	
What kind of job are you looking for? What kind of job are you interested in? What would be your perfect/ideal job?	I'm looking for a full-time/part-time job with good pay. I'd like a job with a retirement plan and health insurance. I want to work for a company that has good training programs. I want to go/work freelance. I want to be my own boss.

Talk 1

Discuss the questions with your partner.

1. Talk about a job that you have had. What did you like and dislike about it?
2. What would be your ideal job? Give reasons for your choice.
3. What would be the worst kind of job for you?

Example

A: Have you ever had a job?
B: Yes, I worked part-time as a waitress.
A: What did you like about it?
B: I liked meeting lots of different kinds of people.
A: And what did you dislike about it?
⋮

Dialogue 2 *Listen to the dialogue and practice.*

Ms Lee:	Thank you for coming to today's interview, Paula.
Paula:	It's a pleasure for me to be here. Thank you for inviting me.
Mr Jones:	Let's start by looking at your resume in more detail. How long have you worked as an editor?
Paula:	I've worked as an editor since I graduated. I've worked at Birdhouse Press for four years now.
Ms Lee:	Do you have any experience of working on electronic products?
Paula:	Yes, I do. I've worked on a number of web and mobile applications. That's why I want to work for your company. I want to work more on electronic products and develop my skills in that area.
Mr Jones:	OK, good. And what would you say are your strengths and weaknesses?
Paula:	I think my main strength is project management. As for my weakness … I'm a perfectionist, so sometimes I don't know when to stop working on a project.

Comprehension Check!

1. How long has Paula worked as an editor?
2. How long has Paula worked at Birdhouse Press?
3. What are Paula's strengths and weaknesses?

Language Focus 2

Talking about Work Experience	
How long have you worked as an editor? How long have you been an editor?	I've worked as an editor **since** I graduated / **since** 2007 / **for** four years. I've been an editor **since** I graduated / **since** 2010 / **for** four years.
Do you have any experience of working **on** electronic products?	Yes, I do. I've worked on electronic products. No, I don't. I haven't worked on electronic products.
What are your strengths and weaknesses? What would you say are your strengths and weaknesses?	I think my main strength is project management. As for my weakness, I'm a perfectionist.

Talk 2

A Ask three classmates questions to complete the table. Ask questions with *how long* using the verbs in the table.

Verbs	Classmate 1	Classmate 2	Classmate 3
live in			
know (someone)			
work			
own			

Example
A: How long have you lived in Seoul?
B: I've lived in Seoul for 18 years / since I was born.

B Tell the class what you found out about your other classmates.

Pronunciation

Intonation in Questions

Discover Pronunciation!

Listen to the extracts from **Dialogue 2**. Notice how the speakers' voices rise or fall when they ask questions.

Mr Jones: How long have you worked as an editor? ↘
Paula: I've worked as an editor since I graduated.

Ms Lee: Do you have any experience of working on electronic products? ↗
Paula: Yes, I do.

When the answer to a question can be *yes* or *no*, the speaker's voice rises (↗). When the question is open, and *yes* or *no* cannot be the answer, the speaker's voice falls (↘).

Practice Pronunciation!

A Read the dialogue. Decide whether the speakers' voices should rise or fall after each question. Write ↗ or ↘ in each gap.

A: What kind of job are you looking for? ____
B: I'm looking for a job in a bank.

A: Do you want to work in a city? ____
B: Yes, I want to work in a city.

A: Do you have any experience of working in a bank? ____
B: Yes, I do.

A: How long have you worked in a bank? ____
B: Almost five years.

B Practice the dialogue in **A** with your partner, using your own personal information.

Talk 3

A Divide the class into two groups. One group will be job applicants. The other group will be recruiters. Discuss with your group what skills and experience are needed for each job.

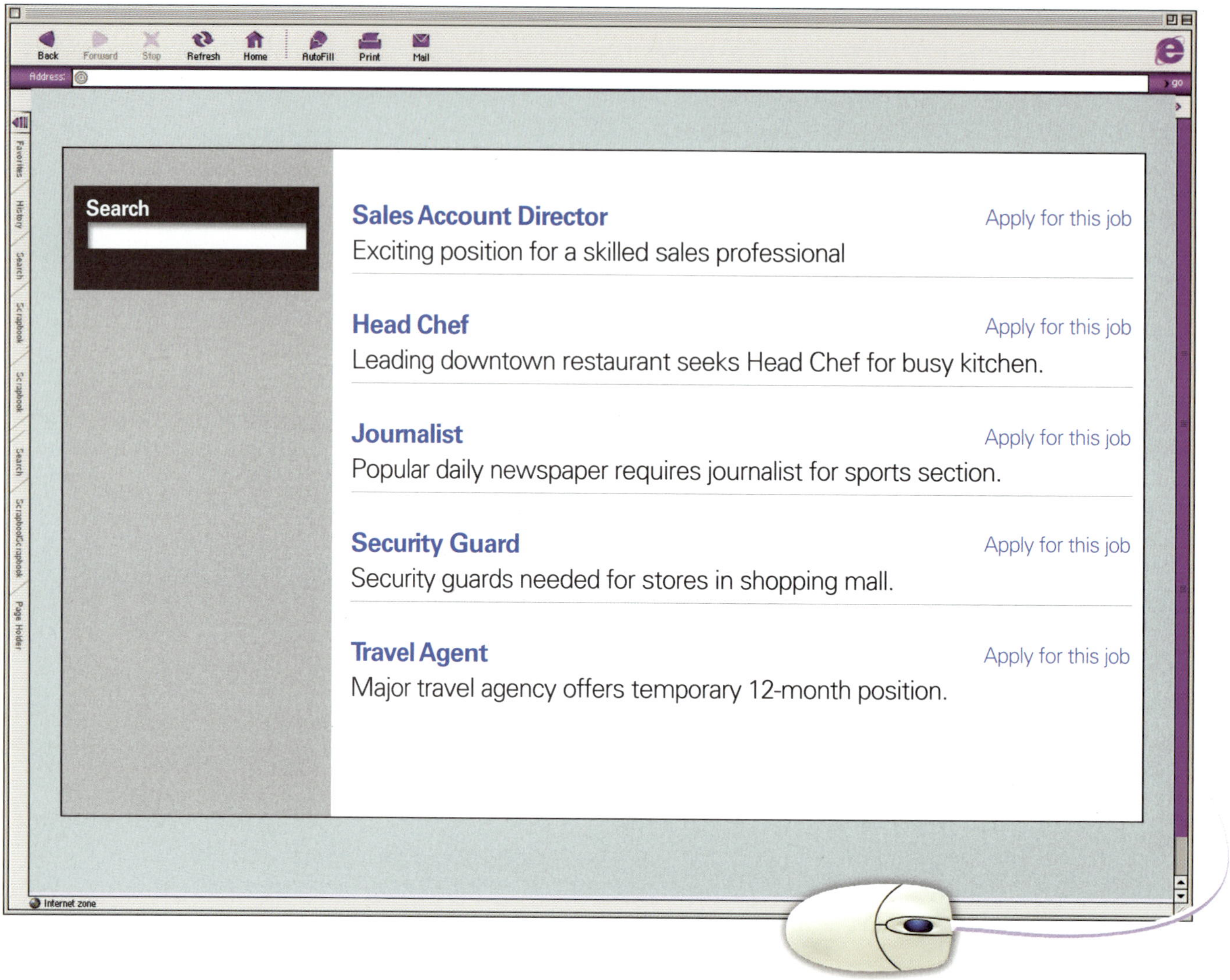

Back
Forward
Stop
Refresh
Home
AutoFill
Print
Mail
Address:
go
Favorites
History
Search
Scrapbook
Page Holder
Search
Sales Account Director
Apply for this job
Exciting position for a skilled sales professional
Head Chef
Apply for this job
Leading downtown restaurant seeks Head Chef for busy kitchen.
Journalist
Apply for this job
Popular daily newspaper requires journalist for sports section.
Security Guard
Apply for this job
Security guards needed for stores in shopping mall.
Travel Agent
Apply for this job
Major travel agency offers temporary 12-month position.
Internet zone

B Roleplay interviews for the jobs. Then decide who is the best person for each job.

Example

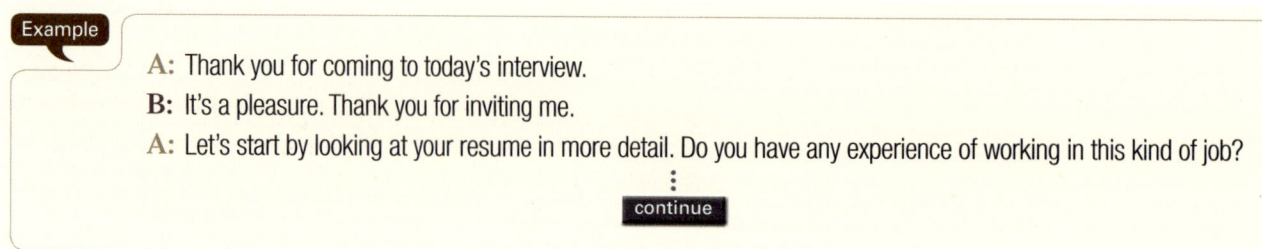

A: Thank you for coming to today's interview.
B: It's a pleasure. Thank you for inviting me.
A: Let's start by looking at your resume in more detail. Do you have any experience of working in this kind of job?
⋮
continue

i Read

A Read the common interview questions. Which do you think are the most difficult to answer?

B Discuss the questions with your partner.

1. How would you answer each of the questions in **A**?
2. Have you ever been to an interview? How did it go?

i Write

A Write a resume, using your own personal information.

RESUME

Personal Information
Name:
Contact details:

Education

Work Experience

Skills

Awards

Hobbies/Interests

B Roleplay job interviews with your partner, using your resumes in **A**.

Lesson 12
What do you enjoy about your job?

Warm-Up

A Match the work activities with the pictures.

| go on business trips | use the Internet | manage people |
| attend meetings | visit clients | give presentations |

B Discuss the questions with your partner.
1. Have you done any of the work activities in **A**? What did you like about them?
2. Which of the work activities in **A** would you like to do more often? Which wouldn't you like to do? Give reasons.

Dialogue 1
Listen to the dialogue and practice.

Penny: So, Oscar, how is your job going?
Oscar: Well, I still have a lot to learn, but I'm enjoying it.
Penny: What do you enjoy about it?
Oscar: I enjoy visiting clients. I like getting out of the office. I really dislike staying inside all day. What about you? Are you enjoying your job?
Penny: Well, I'm tired of going on business trips. Almost every week I go somewhere. I spent the last three weeks in Italy without a break. I'm exhausted!
Oscar: Yes, that sounds kind of extreme. Is there anything that you like about the job?
Penny: Yes, there are things that I like. I enjoy giving presentations. I also like attending meetings with co-workers from around the world. It's exciting and interesting.
Oscar: Yes, it must be. I try to avoid going to meetings in my company as they are kind of boring!

Comprehension Check!

1. What do Penny and Oscar like about their jobs? Why?
2. What do Penny and Oscar dislike about their jobs? Why?

Language Focus 1

Talking about Likes and Dislikes

What do you like about you job? **What do you enjoy about** your job?	**I like** gett**ing** out of the office. **I like** giv**ing** presentations. **I enjoy** visit**ing** clients. **I enjoy** attend**ing** meetings.
What do you dislike about your job? **What do you not enjoy about** your job?	**I dislike** stay**ing** inside all day. **I don't enjoy** attend**ing** meetings. **I'm tired of** go**ing** on business trips.

Talk 1

A Ask three classmates the questions and write the responses.

❶ What do you enjoy doing?

Classmate 1 _____
Classmate 2 _____
Classmate 3 _____

❷ What do you dislike doing?

Classmate 1 _____
Classmate 2 _____
Classmate 3 _____

❸ What are you tired of doing?

Classmate 1 _____
Classmate 2 _____
Classmate 3 _____

B Tell the class what you found out about your partner.

> **Example**
> I found out that Sarah enjoys going on business trips. She dislikes ··· `continue`

Dialogue 2
Listen to the dialogue and practice.

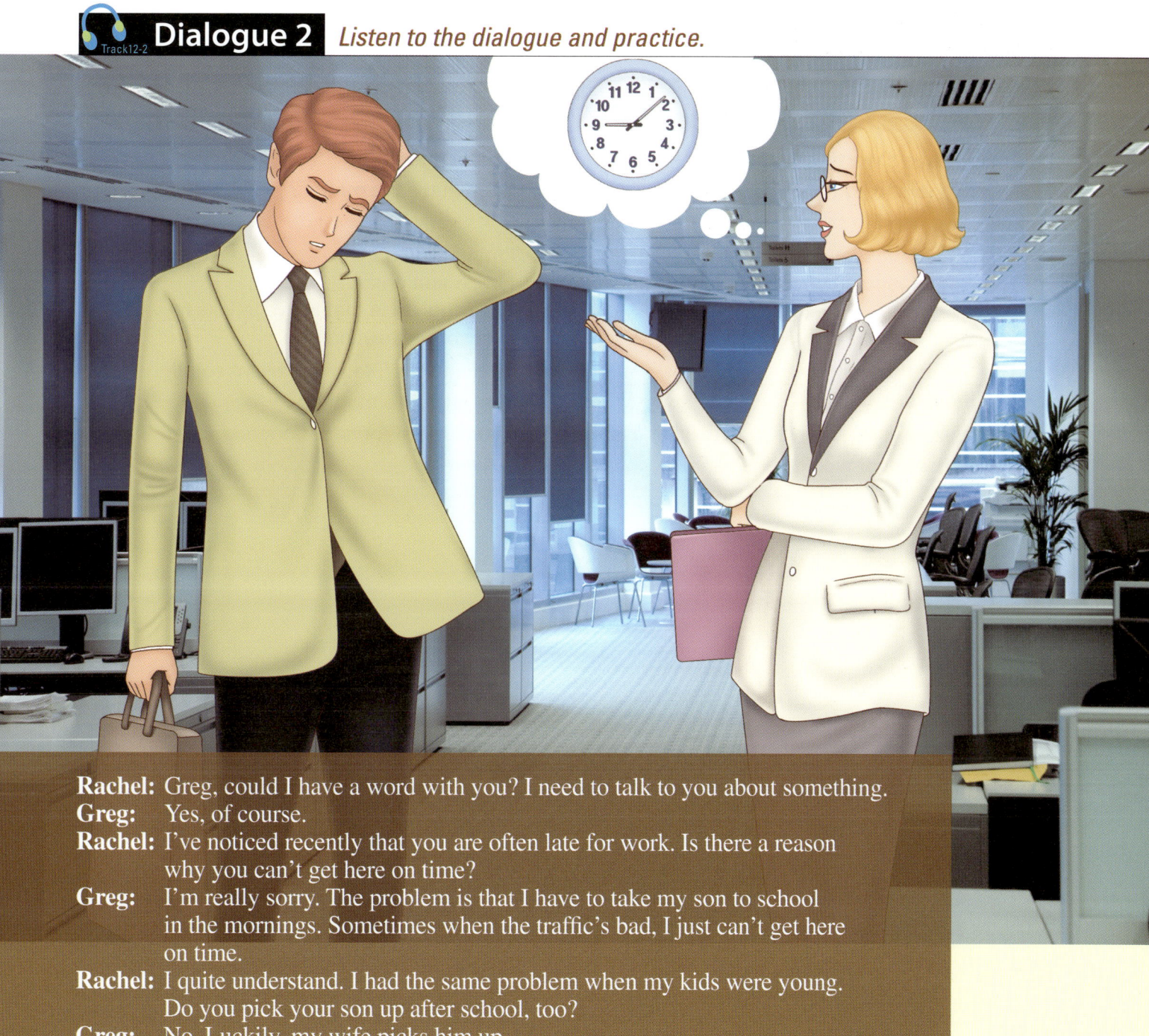

Rachel: Greg, could I have a word with you? I need to talk to you about something.
Greg: Yes, of course.
Rachel: I've noticed recently that you are often late for work. Is there a reason why you can't get here on time?
Greg: I'm really sorry. The problem is that I have to take my son to school in the mornings. Sometimes when the traffic's bad, I just can't get here on time.
Rachel: I quite understand. I had the same problem when my kids were young. Do you pick your son up after school, too?
Greg: No. Luckily, my wife picks him up.
Rachel: Then how about this solution? Let's change your working hours to 9:30 to 5:30. That way you won't have to rush in the mornings, and you won't be late. Do you think that would help?
Greg: That sounds like an excellent solution. Thanks a lot for your understanding.
Rachel: No problem.

Comprehension Check!

1. What problem are Rachel and Greg discussing?
2. What solution does Rachel suggest?

Language Focus 2

Discussing Problems at Work	
Could I have a word with you? I need to talk to you about something. I think we need to talk.	Yes, of course. OK. What's the matter?
I've noticed that you are often late for work. **Is there a reason why** you are often late for work?	I'm really sorry. I must apologize. **The problem is that** I have to take my son to school in the mornings.
How about this solution? Why don't we try this? **Let's** change your working hours to 9:30 to 5:30. Do you think that would help?	That sounds like an excellent solution. Yes, let's give that a try. Thanks a lot for your understanding.

Talk 2

 Match the situations with the responses.

① A co-worker invites you to have dinner, but you don't want to go.
② You arrive late for a meeting.
③ A co-worker tells you some bad news about themselves.
④ Your co-worker ignores you whenever you say 'hello' to her.
⑤ You spill coffee over your boss's desk.
⑥ You can hear your co-worker's music through his earphones.

ⓐ 'I must apologize for being late.'
ⓑ 'I'm really sorry for the mess.'
ⓒ 'I've noticed that you never speak to me.'
ⓓ 'I'm really sorry, but I can't.'
ⓔ 'Excuse me. Could you turn down the music?'
ⓕ 'I'm so sorry to hear that.'

B Roleplay the situations in **A** with your partner.

> Example
> **A:** I must apologize for being late.
> **B:** Yes, I've noticed that you're often late. Is there a reason?
> continue

Pronunciation

-n't

Discover Pronunciation!
Listen to the sentences. Notice how the speaker stresses *can't*.

I **can** get here on time.   *I* **can't** get here on time.

Verbs with the negative ending *-n't* are always stressed, even when they are auxiliary verbs.

Practice Pronunciation!

A Listen and check (✓) the sentence that you hear, **a** or **b**.
1. ⓐ Are you free?   ⓑ Aren't you free?
2. ⓐ I can help you.   ⓑ I can't help you.
3. ⓐ We were happy.   ⓑ We weren't happy.
4. ⓐ She can swim.   ⓑ She can't swim.
5. ⓐ They were running.   ⓑ They weren't running.

B Practice saying the sentences in **A** with your partner. Does your partner know which sentence you are saying?

Talk 3

Discuss with your partner what you would say and do in each difficult work situation.
1. Your co-worker got promoted, but you didn't.
2. Your boss takes credit for your work.
3. Your boss doesn't give you any guidance.
4. You know that you're going to miss a deadline.

i Read

A Read the posts from an internet careers forum. What job does each person have?

Do you like your job?
If you do, why do you like it?

ANSWERS

Answer from Jacobelli

Yes, I work as a researcher in a university, and I enjoy planning my own work.
In my job, I have to work independently. I like choosing my own research projects and doing the work myself. Sometimes I dislike being alone all the time in the laboratory, but generally it's OK.

Answer from shooting star

Yes, I like my job.
I think my job's great. I work at a busy downtown restaurant. I enjoy meeting customers from around the world. I like working in the evenings, because then I have some free time during the day. Sometimes I get tired of standing up all evening, but usually I feel fine. I especially like eating the free food that we get every evening, cooked by our award-winning chef. Delicious!

Answer from Hewings

Yes, my job is very enjoyable.
I find my job as a business consultant very enjoyable. I like working with clients to help them solve their business issues. I really enjoy solving problems, so it's the ideal job for me. I'm also quite a competitive person, so I like working to help my company be better than our competitors. I kind of dislike traveling all the time to visit clients, but that's just the nature of the job!

B Discuss the questions with your partner.

1. What do the people in **A** like and dislike about their jobs?
2. Which of the jobs in **A** would you prefer? Why?

i Write

A What do you like and dislike in your work/studies and in your private life? Make notes.

B Write a short paragraph about your likes and dislikes, using the information in **A**.

Lesson 13

I want to go somewhere special.

Warm-Up

A What do you like to do on vacation? Check (✓) the activities that you like.

☐ go to the beach   ☐ take a cruise   ☐ go cross-country skiing

☐ go on safari   ☐ go camping   ☐ take a bus tour

B Where is the best place to do each activity? Complete the sentences, using your own ideas.

I'd like to	go to the beach	in
	go cross-country skiing	
	go on safari	
	go camping	
	take a cruise	
	take a bus tour	

Dialogue 1 — Listen to the dialogue and practice.

Sean: Marie, where do you want to go for our winter vacation?
Marie: Well, I want to go somewhere special, like the Ice Hotel in Sweden.
Sean: Ice Hotel? Are you saying it's made of real ice?
Marie: It sure is! It's made of snow and ice. It melts and turns into water in spring.
Sean: How interesting! Where can we sleep? In an ice room?!
Marie: Yes, actually! Guests sleep on beds built of snow and ice. We'll need to wear thermal underwear and a hat.
Sean: Amazing! How cold is the room?
Marie: They say it's about minus five degrees Celsius! Everything in the room, such as the furniture and sculptures, is made of ice.
Sean: It sounds so fascinating! Let's start planning our vacation right now.
Marie: Sounds good to me!

Comprehension Check!

1. What is the Ice Hotel made of?
2. When do you think Sean and Marie will go on vacation?

Language Focus 1

Expressing Interest	
The hotel is made of snow and ice.	How interesting! Amazing! It sounds so fascinating!

Talk 1

Complete the chart and discuss your best and worst vacation with your partner.

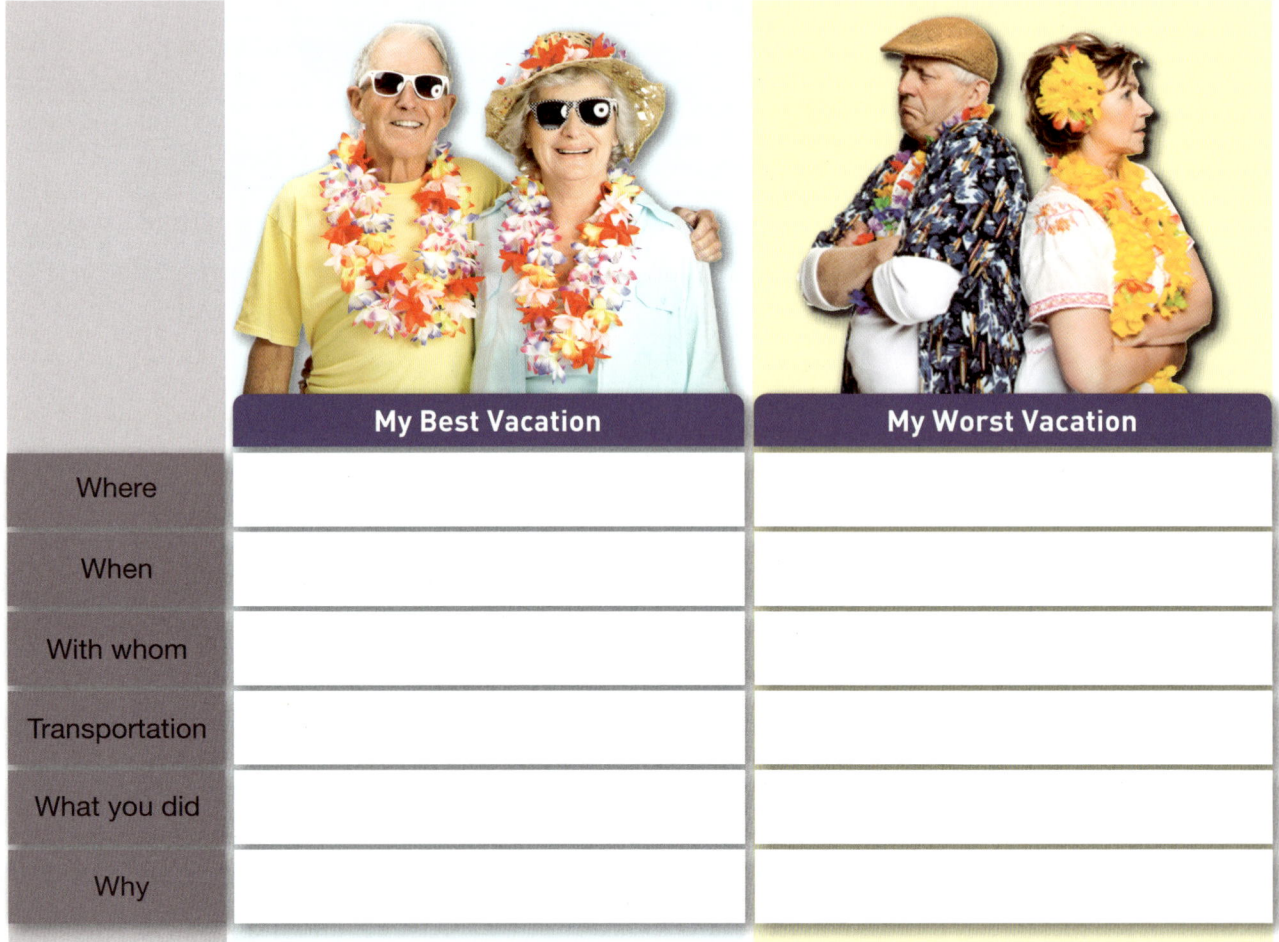

	My Best Vacation	My Worst Vacation
Where		
When		
With whom		
Transportation		
What you did		
Why		

Example
Q: What was your best/worst vacation?
A: My best/worst vacation was when I went to ··· continue

Pronunciation

/r/ and /l/

Discover Pronunciation!

When we pronounce /r/, the tip of the tongue curls back without touching the top of the mouth.
When we pronounce /l/, the tip of the tongue touches the top teeth.

Practice Pronunciation!

A Listen to the words and practice saying them.

1. rate / late
2. right / light
3. rice / lice
4. race / lace
5. berry / belly
6. pray / play
7. crash / clash
8. Rick / lick
9. correct / collect

B Practice saying the tongue twisters. Work with your partner.

1. Roberta ran rings around the Roman ruins.

2. Clean clams crammed in clean cans.

3. Luke Luck likes lakes.
   Luke's duck likes lakes.
   Luke Luck licks lakes.
   Luck's duck licks lakes.
   Duck takes licks in lakes Luke Luck likes.
   Luke Luck takes licks in lakes ducks like.

4. Lick the red lolly, lick the yellow lolly.
   Red lorry, yellow lorry.
   Laura and Larry rarely lull their rural roosters to sleep.
   Jerry's berry jelly really rankled his broiling belly.
   Collecting the corrections is the role of the elderly.

Dialogue 2 *Listen to the dialogue and practice.*

Steve: Hi, Angela! When did you get back from Bali?
Angela: Hey, Steve! I just got back yesterday.
Steve: You look very refreshed. How was the trip?
Angela: It was so wonderful! Our family rented a private villa. We had a private driver, a butler, a chef, and even an in-house spa therapist!
Steve: Wow! It sounds like a dream vacation!
Angela: That's not all. I swam in our private swimming pool and got beauty treatments everyday.
Steve: Sounds relaxing. How about the food? Did you have any traditional Balinese cuisine?
Angela: Of course I did. The chef cooked really delicious steamed rice, meat, and vegetables. She also made some western food.
Steve: I think my family would love to have a vacation like that. But wasn't it really expensive?
Angela: We went on a special package deal, so it wasn't too bad. If you're interested, I'll give you the information.
Steve: Yes, please. I'd appreciate that.

Comprehension Check!

1. What was special about the private villa in Bali?
2. What do you think Steve will do?

Language Focus 2

Talking about Vacations	
When did you get back from Bali?	I just got back yesterday. I came back last week.
How was your trip?	It was so wonderful! It was incredible! It was boring.

 Talk 2

🎧 Listen to two people talking about vacations in their countries and complete the table, using the words from the box.

	Tamara	Ahmed
Country		
Places to Go		
Things to See/Do		
Food		

Cancun	Mexico	Turkey
Cappadocia	Chichen Itza	white sands, clear water
enjoy the sunshine	hot air ballooning	tacos, tortillas, peppers
kebabs, pilaf, Turkish coffee, meze	rock-cut churches, monasteries	well-preserved frescoes

Talk 3

Ask and answer the questions with your partner.

A: Where are you going for your vacation?
B:
A: What are you going to do there?
B:
A: What kind of food do they have there?
B:

i Read

A Read the advertisement for vacation packages. Which package would you choose?

DISCOUNT TRAVEL AGENCY

* Special Offers

Caribbean Package Deals

SAVE UP TO **70%**! → Learn More

- Big City Tours
- Big Savings on Las Vegas Vacations
- Big Savings on Disneyland Vacations
- New York City Package Deals
- Save on European Flight + Hotel Packages
- Last Minute Package Deals

Save Up to 45%!
One-Day Sale!
Save Up to 40%!
Exclusive Prices!
Save Up to 40%!
Up to $100 Free Spending Money!

Top Destinations	Interests and Ideas
Caribbean	All Inclusive Vacations
Mexico	Family Vacations
Hawaii	Honeymoon Vacations
Europe	Beach Vacations
Canada	Theme Park Vacations

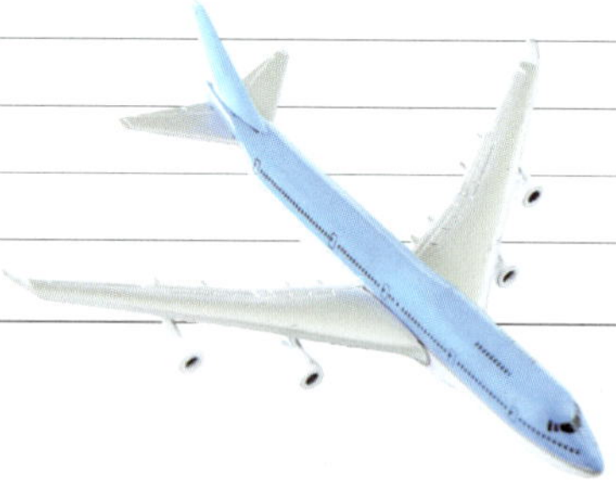

B Discuss the questions with your partner.

1. Which package has the biggest discount?
2. How much can you save if you take the Disneyland vacation package?

i Write

Complete the survey, referring to the information in *i* **Read**.

Dream Vacation Survey

1. How many people will be going on the vacation?
   Number of Adults _____
   Number of Children _____

2. Where do you want to go? Choose three from the 'Top Destinations' list.
   1) _____
   2) _____
   3) _____

3. What kind of vacation do you want? Choose three from the 'Interests and Ideas' list.
   1) _____
   2) _____
   3) _____

4. Which special offers are you interested in? Choose three from the 'Special Offers' list.
   1) _____
   2) _____
   3) _____

5. What is most important to you in a vacation?
   _____

Thank You.

Lesson 14
I downloaded some apps for my smartphone.

Warm-Up

A Which of the high-tech devices do you use? How often do you use them? What do you use them for?

mobile apps | laptop | digital camera | smart TV

B Discuss the questions with your partner.
1. How important is technology in your life?
2. Does technology have a good or bad effect on our lives?

Dialogue 1 — Listen to the dialogue and practice.

Christina: Marco, you look so tired!
Marco: Yes, I've been up all night reading these books. I'm so worried about the exam next week. I always do so badly in exams!
Christina: Hmm … I think you need to practice your exam technique. Just studying books isn't enough.
Marco: Sure. But how can I do that?
Christina: Well, I downloaded some exam practice apps for my smartphone. With the apps, I can practice the exam with a timer, and also get tips on each question.
Marco: Wow, that sounds great! How can I get those apps?
Christina: First, go to the app store on your smartphone. Then, search for the name of the exam. When you see the exam apps, just press 'download'. That's it!
Marco: OK, I'll do that. Thanks for your advice, Christina.

Comprehension Check!

① What is Marco worried about?
② What does Christina advise?

Language Focus 1

Explaining How to Use Technology

How can I download exam practice apps? **How do you** download exam practice apps? **What's the best way to** download exam practice apps?	**First,** go to the app store on your smartphone. **Then,** search for the name of the exam. **When you** see the exam apps, just press 'download'. **That's it!**

Talk 1

Talk with your partner about how to do each thing.

send a text message

change the security code on an electronic door lock

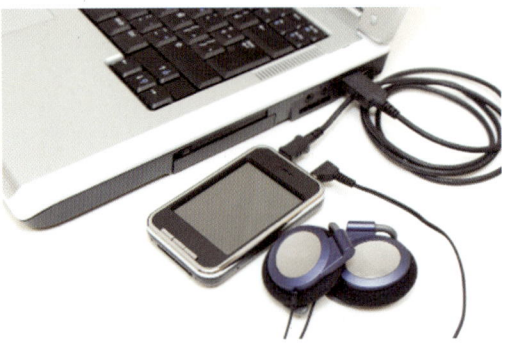

download music onto an MP3 player

use a computer to control your personal budget

Example

A: What's the best way to download music onto an MP3 player?
B: First, connect the MP3 player to a computer. Then, ··· `continue`

Dialogue 2
Listen to the dialogue and practice.

Hannah: Grandpa, why don't I buy you a cell phone? That way we can always contact you, and you can contact us whenever you need to.
Desmond: A cell phone?! No, thank you. I don't know how to use a cell phone.
Hannah: Cell phones are simple to use. I'll show you how to use it.
Desmond: I'm perfectly happy with our house phone. I don't need anything else.
Hannah: But, grandpa, the advantage of a cell phone is that you can take it with you wherever you go.
Desmond: But doesn't it use a lot of electricity?
Hannah: No. You just charge the phone up every two days or so. Then you can take it with you when you go out. That's why I think you should have a cell phone.
Desmond: I don't need to contact anyone when I go out!
Hannah: Oh, grandpa. We just want you to be safe. Cell phones are useful for staying in touch when you go out.
Desmond: I know. Thank you, dear. But my biggest concern is that your grandmother would be able to call me wherever I am!
Hannah: Well, that's a good point!

Comprehension Check!
1. What does Hannah want to do for Desmond?
2. Why does Desmond refuse Hannah's offer?

Language Focus 2

Persuading

Grandpa, **why don't I** buy you a cell phone**? That way** we can always contact you, and you can contact us whenever you need to.

The advantage of a cell phone **is that** you can take it with your wherever you go.

That's why I think you should have a cell phone.

Cell phones **are useful for** stay**ing** in touch when you go out.

Cell phones **are simple to use**.

Rejecting Persuasion

No, thank you. I don't know how to use a cell phone.

But doesn't it use a lot of electricity**?**

My biggest concern is that your grandmother **would** be able to call me wherever I am!

Pronunciation

Exclamations

Discover Pronunciation!
Listen to the extracts from **Dialogue 1** and **Dialogue 2**.

Marco, you look so tired!
I always do so badly in exams!
Wow, that sounds great!
I don't need to contact anyone when I go out!
Well, that's a good point!

When we make exclamations (!), our intonation rises.

Practice Pronunciation!
Practice saying the sentences with your partner.

1. Look out!
2. You look fantastic!
3. That's my pen!
4. Oh no!
5. This is a disaster!

Talk 2

A Match the high-tech devices with their older equivalents.

1.  laptop
2.  e-book reader
3.  sat nav
4.  webcam
5.  robotic vacuum cleaner

a.  map
b.  vacuum cleaner
c.  telephone
d.  typewriter
e.  book

B Roleplay conversations with your partner. Try to persuade your partner to use the high-tech devices rather than the older equivalents.

A: Why don't you buy an e-book reader?
B: I'm very happy with my books. Why would I want an e-book reader?
A: Well, the advantage of an e-book reader is that ··· continue

Talk 3

Discuss the questions with your partner.

1. Do you use any of the high-tech devices in **Talk 2**? What do you like/dislike about using them?
2. Do you think it is important for older people to learn how to use technology? Why / Why not?
3. Do you think society depends too much on technology? Why / Why not?

i Read

A Read the posts from an internet forum about the best inventions of all time. Which invention does each person think is the best?

What's the best invention of all time?

The world is now a small place. We can live and work anywhere, and communicate with colleagues, customers, friends, and family around the world. How? Thanks to the telephone! Telephones are simple for everyone to use, and they have completely changed our lives. That's why I think the telephone is the best invention ever.
Nelly_1 July 15, 15:08

I think radio is the best invention of all time. Radio was the first form of mass broadcasting. It brought news and information to people. During difficult periods, such as war, governments could use it to communicate with the people. For me, there is no doubt that the radio is a really important invention.
summerdaze July 15, 15:33

Television – it attracts people's attention like nothing else. The advantage of television over radio is that it uses image and sound. So, that's why I think television is better than radio, and the best invention of all time.
omniamundis July 15, 16:42

B Discuss the questions with your partner.

1. Which of the three inventions in **A** do you think is the best? Why?
2. What do you think is the best invention of all time? Give reasons for your choice.

i Write

A Make notes about each of the inventions. Why is each one important?

Best Inventions?	Reasons
the toilet	• • •
the printing press	• • •
antibiotics	• • •
the use of electricity	• • •
the computer	• • •
the telescope	• • •
the lightbulb	• • •
other:	• •

B Write a short paragraph about one of the inventions **A**, saying why it is the best invention of all time.

Lesson 15

I'm against the idea.

Warm-Up

Complete the table with the pros and cons of online shopping, fast food, and internet dating.

What's Your Opinion?

	Online Shopping	Fast Food	Internet Dating
Pros (Advantages)	• You can do it 24/7.	• You don't have to wait too long.	• You can meet new people easily.
	•	•	•
	•	•	•
	•	•	•
Cons (Disadvantages)	• You can't check the item, or try it on.	• It is fattening.	• Some people lie about themselves.
	•	•	•
	•	•	•
	•	•	•

Dialogue 1 — Listen to the dialogue and practice.

Jack: Kate, I'm so hungry. Let's go to Super Burger.
Kate: You want a hamburger? In that case, no thanks. I don't eat fast food.
Jack: You don't? How come? I love hamburgers with French fries. There's nothing like fast food when you don't have much time.
Kate: Yes, but it's so unhealthy. It contains a lot of fat, salt, and calories.
Jack: Yes, that's true, but as long as you don't eat it everyday, you'll be fine.
Kate: I don't agree. Fast food will make you put on weight. Then you'll get high blood pressure and heart problems.
Jack: I see what you mean, but that's not a problem for me. I exercise regularly. I like fast food because it saves time and money.
Kate: I take your point, but you still need to be careful with fast food.
Jack: You could be right. I think I'll eat less fast food from now on. And I'll eat salads for lunch.
Kate: Sounds great. Then I will come with you for lunch!

Comprehension Check!

1. What is the main topic of the dialogue?
2. Why is Kate against fast food?

Language Focus 1

Discussing Opinions

Yes, but they are so unhealthy.
Yes, that's quite true, but I'll be fine.
I see what you mean, but that's not a problem.
I take your point, but you need to be careful with fast food.
You could be right. I think I'll eat less fast food.

 Pronunciation

Can and Can't

Discover Pronunciation!

Can	Can't

• Usually the vowel is not pronounced. It sounds like the ending of chi<u>cken</u>.
 	
  I can [kən] dance.
 	
• In short answers, can is stressed.
 	
  Yes, I can [kæn].
	• The vowel is stressed and pronounced strongly and clearly.
	
	  I can't [kænt] dance.

Practice Pronunciation!
Practice singing the song. Pay attention to your pronunciation of *can* and *can't*.

There's nothing you **can** do that **can't** be done.
Nothing you **can** sing that **can't** be sung.
Nothing you **can** say but you **can** learn how to play the game.
It's easy.

Nothing you **can** make that **can't** be made.
No one you **can** save that **can't** be saved.
Nothing you **can** do but you **can** learn how to be you in time.
It's easy.
All you need is love.

Talk 1

Complete the sentences, using the expressions from **Language Focus 1**. Then practice with your partner.

A: I love potato chips and soda. They taste great together.
B: _____.

A: You've got to have French fries with hamburgers. You need vegetables.
B: _____.

A: I don't have any time to cook. I have to eat microwave dinners.
B: _____.

Dialogue 2
Listen to the dialogue and practice.

Jenny: Miguel, I've been thinking about our plan to go to the Grand Canyon. I think we'd better change the plan.
Miguel: You were all for the idea until last night! What changed your mind?
Jenny: Well, I'm against the idea for a few reasons. First of all, we're planning to stay in a hotel in Phoenix, right? It's going to be very hot.
Miguel: Yes, but we'll leave for the Grand Canyon early in the morning and come back in the evening. The Grand Canyon isn't so hot.
Jenny: Yes, that's quite true, but it'll take about four hours to get there from the hotel. We'll be exhausted. I think we should go to Hawaii. In Hawaii, you walk out of the hotel, and you're on the beach.
Miguel: I agree, but we can't afford a trip to Hawaii. The flights and hotels would be much more expensive.
Jenny: You're right, but it's our vacation. I'd like to relax and enjoy the trip. I don't want to worry about the weather and the long ride.
Miguel: All right. Let's check on special deals on Hawaiian vacation packages. Then we can decide what to do.
Jenny: Agreed. Thank you. You're so sweet.

Comprehension Check!
1. Why is Jenny against going to the Grand Canyon?
2. What does Miguel suggest?

Language Focus 2

Discussing Ideas

You were all for the idea until last night!
I'm against the idea for a few reasons.
We can't afford a trip to Hawaii.

Talk 2

Listen to the dialogue and practice.

Clara: Let's spend our vacation at a luxury resort this summer. It would be really relaxing.
Mike: Well, I'm against the idea. I'd prefer to go backpacking around Europe or some tropical countries. It would be cheap and fun.
Clara: I see what you mean, but I just want to have a break from my busy life. I need a good massage, delicious meals, and beautiful views.
Mike: I take your point, but I don't think we can afford it.

For or **Against**?

Talk 3

Listen to the dialogue and answer the questions.

1. What is the main topic of the dialogue?
2. What does Sean expect from the new doughnut shop?
3. What does Kate want to buy?

i Read

A Read the article about milk. What are the pros and cons of drinking milk?

Quick Survey on Milk

1. What kind of milk do you prefer?
   - a non-fat
   - b low-fat
   - c whole
   - d soy
   - e artificially flavored

2. When do you drink milk?
   - a breakfast
   - b lunch
   - c dinner
   - d snack time
   - e before going to bed

3. How much milk do you drink per week?

4. Why do you drink milk?

5. Which brand do you prefer?

'Milk Does Your Body Good' — Does It?

For a long time, we've been told that milk is good for our bodies. However, some recent studies show that drinking milk has cons as well as pros.

•• Arguments about Milk

Pros

It is rich in calcium and vitamin D. It can lower your cancer risk.

It can speed up weight loss. It helps burn body fat.

Skimmed milk is low in saturated fat. It is a good source of protein.

It strengthens bones. This is particularly important for teenagers.

Cons

High levels of growth hormone IGF-1 stimulate cancer cells.

There is no strong evidence that it helps people lose weight.

Whole milk is high in saturated fat. Also, milk is a common cause of food allergy.

It doesn't have a huge effect on bone health. Healthy bones depend on physical activity.

B Discuss the questions with your partner.

1. Do you drink milk regularly? Why do you drink it?
2. Which arguments do you agree and disagree with?

i Write

Complete the sentences, referring to *i* Read.

Arguments about Milk

- It can _____ weight loss. It helps burn _____.
- It is rich in calcium and vitamin D. It can _____.
- It _____ bones. This is particularly important for teenagers.
- Skimmed milk is low in saturated fat. It is a good _____.

- There is no strong _____ that it helps people lose weight.
- Whole milk is high in _____ fat. Also, milk is a common cause of food _____.
- It doesn't have a huge effect on bone health. Healthy bones _____ physical activity.
- High levels of _____ IGF-1 _____ cancer cells.

Lesson 16
I'd probably ask him for his autograph.

Warm-Up

A Match the sentence beginnings to the correct endings.

❶  If I were rich,		ⓐ I would build new apartments for everyone. 
❷  If I could live anywhere in the world,		ⓑ I would write a novel. 
❸  If I had more free time,		ⓒ I would propose to her. 
❹  If I were President,		ⓓ I would buy a sports car. 
❺  If I had a girlfriend,		ⓔ I would live in Hawaii. 

B Talk with your partner about what you would do in the situations in **A**. Complete the sentences.

❶ If I were rich, I would _____. My partner would _____.
❷ If I could live anywhere in the world, I would _____.
   My partner would _____.
❸ If I had more free time, I would _____. My partner would _____.
❹ If I were President, I would _____. My partner would _____.

Dialogue 1 — Listen to the dialogue and practice.

Paul: Guess what! Yesterday I met Tony Jackson!
Jenny: You mean Tony Jackson, the actor? Wow! Where did you meet him?
Paul: He came to my company's anniversary party.
Jenny: Oh, I see. So what did you say to him?
Paul: Actually, I didn't say anything. I didn't know what to say to him!
Jenny: Oh, so you didn't actually *meet* him!
Paul: Well … I guess not. Have you ever met a celebrity?
Jenny: No, I haven't.
Paul: What would you do if you did?
Jenny: I'd probably ask him for his autograph. But, if I met Tony Jackson …
Paul: Yes? What would you have done if you were me?
Jenny: I'd have taken a photo with him. He's so handsome!
Paul: Whatever!

Comprehension Check!

1. Who did Paul meet? What did he do?
2. What would Jenny have done?

Language Focus 1

Imagined Situations

Have you ever met a celebrity?	Yes, I have. No, I haven't.
What would you do if you did (meet a celebrity)?	(**If** I **met** a celebrity,) **I'd** ask him for his autograph.
What would you have done if you were me?	(**If I were** you,) **I'd have** taken a photo with him.

Talk 1

A Talk with your partner about the situations. Have you ever been in the situations? If you have, what did you do? If you haven't, what would you do?

❶
found some money

❷
been locked out of your house

❸
met a celebrity

❹
lost your cell phone

❺
got lost in a strange place

Example

A: Greg, have you ever met a celebrity?
B: No, I haven't.
A: What would you do if you did?
B: I'd ··· continue

B Tell the class what you found out about your partner.

Dialogue 2
Listen to the dialogue and practice.

Jason: Sunset always makes me think of the future.
Raquel: Me too. Summer's almost over. What are your plans for the future?
Jason: I'm planning to apply to graduate school next year. How about you?
Raquel: Well, I've always dreamt of traveling. I'm going to get a part-time job in the fall to earn some money.
Jason: Sounds good. I'd like to travel, too, but I think I should study more first. I hope to start my own company before I'm 30.
Raquel: My hope is to become a lawyer. I'm planning to study law at graduate school in a few years' time.
Jason: Cool. Do you have any other dreams?
Raquel: Well, I hope to get married and start a family someday.
Jason: Me too. It's exciting, isn't it? We have our whole lives ahead of us.
Raquel: Right. Let's meet here again someday and see how our lives have changed.
Jason: It's a deal!

Comprehension Check!

1. What does Jason hope to do in the future?
2. What are Raquel's hopes?

Language Focus 2

Hopes and Dreams

What do you hope to do in the future?	I hope to start my own company.
What are your hopes for the future?	My hope is to become a lawyer.
Do you have any dreams?	My dream is to travel.
What are your dreams?	I've always dreamt of traveling.
What are your plans for the future?	I'm planning to apply to graduate school.
What are you planning to do after the summer?	I'm going to get a part-time job.

Pronunciation

Pronoun Contractions

Discover Pronunciation!

Listen to the extracts from **Dialogue 1** and **Dialogue 2**. Notice how the speakers say the highlighted words.

I'd probably ask him.

I'm planning to apply.

I've always dreamt of traveling.

I'm going to get a part-time job.

I'd like to travel.

We do not usually stress pronouns or pronoun contractions.

Practice Pronunciation!

A Underline the stressed words in each sentence.

❶ I've finished it.   ❹ We've done it.
❷ I'll ask him.   ❺ She'd help him.
❸ He's seen her.

B Practice saying the sentences in **A**. Pay attention to stress.

Talk 2

A Complete the table with your hopes and dreams for the future in each category.

	5 Years from Now	20 Years from Now
Job		
Romance		
Travel		
Money		

B Talk with your partner about your hopes and dreams for the future. Refer to the information in **A**.

Talk 3

A What do you think will happen to your classmates in the future? Write predictions for four of your classmates.

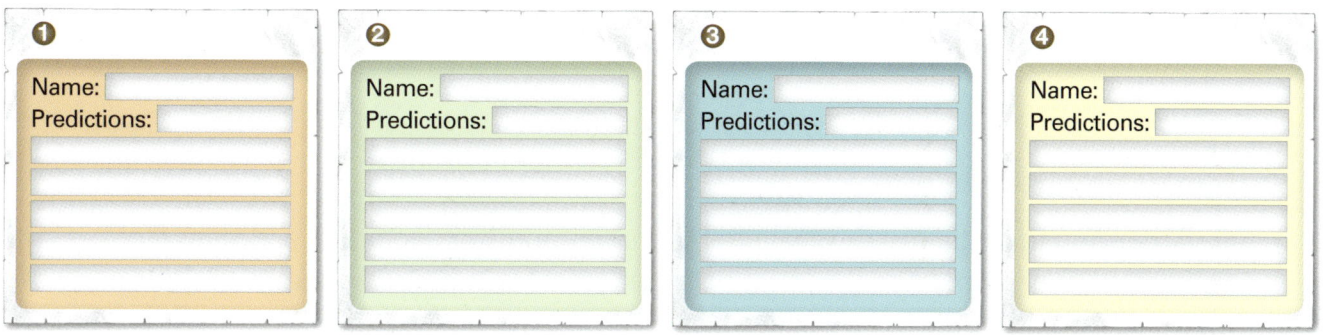

❶ Name: ___ Predictions: ___

❷ Name: ___ Predictions: ___

❸ Name: ___ Predictions: ___

❹ Name: ___ Predictions: ___

B Tell your classmates about your predictions. Do they agree or disagree?

i Read

A Read the following extract from an internet forum about two people's 'dream lives'. Which life would you prefer?

August 10, 13:39   #1

rustic-muse
Full Member
Join Date: Apr 2009
Posts: 97

What would be your 'dream life'?

I think there are three important factors in a 'dream life': house, work, and spouse. If I could build my dream house, I would build it in a large field in the countryside somewhere. It would have large rooms with high ceilings. As far as work is concerned, my dream is to be a farmer. If I were a farmer, I could live a slow and peaceful life. Finally, my dream spouse would be a strong, energetic woman. She would be a farmer like me.

August 11, 09:17   #1

citygirl
Junior Member
Join Date: Jul 2011
Posts: 2

What would be your 'dream life'?

My 'dream life' would be very different to rustic-muse's 'dream life'. If I was rich enough, I'd live in a penthouse in the center of the city. The penthouse would have a swimming pool and sauna, and there would be plenty of space for parties. For my job, I'd be an editor on a fashion magazine. That way, I could meet lots of famous people. Who knows? Maybe I would marry a movie star! That would be a 'dream life' for me.

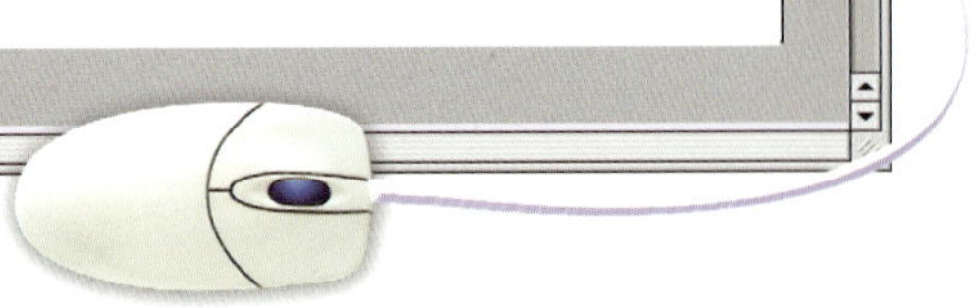

B Discuss the questions with your partner.

1. According to rustic-muse, what are the three important factors in a 'dream life'?
2. For you, what would be the most important factors in a 'dream life'?
3. Do you think a 'dream life' really exists? Why / Why not?

i Write

A Complete the table by asking three classmates about their 'dream lives'. Also, write about your own 'dream life'. Use the words below, or your own ideas.

	You	Classmate 1	Classmate 2	Classmate 3
Dream House				
Dream Job				
Dream Spouse				
Other: _____				

House			
in the city	in the countryside	near the sea	in the mountains
in a small village	on a hill	in a field	by a lake

Job			
farmer	editor	journalist	teacher
actor	musician	accountant	banker

Spouse			
energetic	intelligent	understanding	gentle
beautiful/handsome	strong	rich	outgoing

B Choose one of the 'dream lives' in **A** and write a short paragraph to describe it.

Listening Scripts

Lesson 4

[Talk 2]
Listen to the dialogue and practice.

Emily: Ken, why did you choose to major in history?
Ken: Because I really enjoy learning about the past. I want to be a high school history teacher. How about you?
Emily: I majored in English because I wanted to be a good communicator. English is a global language, so I thought it was the best choice.

Lesson 6

[Talk 2]
Listen to the dialogue and practice.

Situation 1
A: Do you mind if I ask you a personal question?
B: Go ahead.
A: How much are you paid?
B: Half what I'm worth.

Situation 2
A: This might be a bit personal, but I hear you're single.
B: Oh, yeah? When did that happen?

Situation 3
A: I know it's none of my business, but how much did that cost?
B: I got a good deal. It wasn't as much as you'd think.

[Talk 3]
Listen to the dialogue and practice.

A: Why do people ask rude questions? They should know better.
B: You don't have to answer personal questions. Just go about your business.
A: Usually I do. But sometimes they don't give up. It's really annoying.
B: Then tell them it's none of their business.

Lesson 7

[Talk 2]
Listen to the dialogue and practice.

A: Besides taking medication, what do you do if you have a stomachache?
B: I drink peppermint tea. It really works.
A: Besides taking medication, what do you do if you have a cold?
B: I eat chicken soup and rest. That's the best remedy for me.
A: I'm so tired. What do you suggest?
B: Why don't you get a massage? That would be relaxing.

Lesson 9

[Talk 3]
Listen to the dialogue and practice.

Officer: May I help you?
Victim: Yes. I'd like to file a complaint. My car was stolen.
Officer: When did it happen?
Victim: Sometime between yesterday evening and this morning. I parked the car in front of my house around 8:30. When I went outside to get the newspaper this morning, it was gone!

Lesson 10

[Talk 3]
Listen to the dialogue and practice.

Clark: Hey, Janet, what happened to Joe? Why is he in the hospital?
Janet: You haven't heard about the accident, Clark?
Clark: No, I haven't. What accident?
Janet: His car flipped over on Freeway 77.
Clark: Really? How is he? Did he get hurt?
Janet: Luckily, he's doing OK. But his car was beyond the repair. It was totaled.

Lesson 13

[Talk 2]
Listen to two people talking about vacations in their countries and complete the table, using the words from the box.

Mr Miller: Hello, everyone! Welcome to the class. Today, we're going to talk about vacations in different countries. First of all, Tamara, could you tell us about vacations in your country? You can tell us about places to go, food, weather, and so on.

Tamara: All right. There are so many places to go in Mexico. But, if you want to escape from the cold winter and enjoy the sunshine, you need to go to Cancun. Cancun is called 'tourist paradise.' It is known for its beautiful white sands and clear water. You should also visit the Mayan ruins of Chichen Itza. There are good restaurants with Mexican cuisine. Please try authentic tacos, tortillas, and different kinds of peppers.

Mr Miller: Sounds great! Thank you Tamara for sharing. What about you, Ahmed? Could you tell us about vacations in Turkey?

Ahmed: Sure. I invite you to visit Cappadocia. People come to see the underground cities, rock-cut churches, and monasteries. They have well-preserved frescoes. They are considered the best Byzantine art. Also don't miss Cappadocia's hot air ballooning. It is so much fun! As for food, you will love kebabs, pilav, Turkish coffee, and meze.

Mr Miller: Wow! It sounds exciting. I'd love to go to both places. What about you, class? Any questions? Anybody?

Lesson 15

[Talk 2]
Listen to the dialogue and practice.

Clara: Let's spend our vacation at a luxury resort this summer. It would be really relaxing.

Mike: Well, I'm against the idea. I'd prefer to go backpacking around Europe or some tropical countries. It would be cheap and fun.

Clara: I see what you mean, but I just want to have a break from my busy life. I need a good massage, delicious meals, and beautiful views.

Mike: I take your point, but I don't think we can afford it.

[Talk 3]
Listen to the dialogue and answer the questions.

Sean: Kate, did you see the new doughnut shop around the corner? They have an opening sale event!

Kate: Yes! Now we have four doughnut shops in one block. There will be strong competition between them.

Sean: I'm all for it. As they compete, they will offer more discounts and better service.

Kate: You could be right, but what about people's health? Doughnuts are junk food. I want some healthy food to buy!

Sean: You're right, but I'm interested in price. I appreciate any kind of discount. The cheaper the better!

Notes

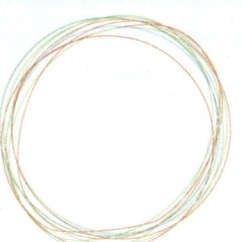

Lesson 1: The disadvantage of Mexico is that it's too hot.

Dialogue 1
Listen to the dialogue and practice.

Travel agent: How can I help you today?
Gina: We'd like to book a vacation.
Travel agent: OK. Where would you like to go?
Gina: We'd like to go somewhere quiet and warm.
Simon: Yes, and somewhere with a good beach.
Travel agent: Perhaps Mexico would be a good destination for you.
Gina: Hmm … the disadvantage of Mexico is that it's too hot.
Simon: Yes, we like warm weather, but not hot weather.
Travel agent: Then how about Florida? A major advantage of Florida is that you can travel there by train. You don't need to fly.
Gina: I think we'd like to go somewhere further away than Florida. We want to go somewhere interesting with lots of things to do, and—
Simon: And, somewhere not too expensive.
Travel agent: OK. Let me take a look at our database and see what we have.

Wordlist

- **destination**
  Mexico would be a good destination for you.
- **disadvantage**
  The disadvantage of Mexico is that it's too hot.
- **advantage**
  A major advantage of Florida is that you can travel there by train.
- **further away**
  We'd like to go somewhere further away than Florida.
- **nervous**
  Flying makes me nervous.
- **turbulence**
  I hate it when there's a lot of turbulence.
- **miss one's flight**
  I always worry about missing my flight.
- **lose one's luggage**
  I also worry about losing my luggage.
- **hijacked**
  My worst fear is that the plane will crash, or be hijacked.
- **switch**
  Shall we switch seats, then?

Dialogue 2 *Listen to the dialogue and practice.*

Isabel: Do you like flying?
William: No, not at all. It makes me nervous. What about you?
Isabel: I feel the same way as you. People often say that flying is safer than driving, but I know which I'd prefer!
William: Yes, I agree. I always worry about bad weather. I hate it when there's a lot of turbulence. It makes me feel sick.
Isabel: I know what you mean. I also worry about missing my flight, or losing my luggage.
William: Yes, I've lost my luggage a few times.
Isabel: My worst fear is that the plane will crash, or be hijacked. What's your worst fear?
William: It's the height that scares me the most. I wish I wasn't sitting next to the window!
Isabel: Shall we switch seats, then?
William: That'd be great. Thanks!

Pronunciation

Syllables

Discover Pronunciation!

English words are made of smaller sounds called *syllables*. Look at the words from **Dialogue 1**:

Help = one syllable
Today = two syllables
Vacation = three syllables

Practice Pronunciation!

A Read the sentences from **Dialogue 1**. How many syllables are there in each sentence? Listen to check your answers.

1. How can I help you today? 7
2. We'd like to book a vacation.
3. Perhaps Mexico would be a good destination for you.
4. The disadvantage of Mexico is that it's too hot.
5. A major advantage of Florida is that you can travel there by train.

B Practice saying the sentences in **A**. Pay attention to the number of syllables.

Lesson 2 — May I see your passport, please?

Dialogue 1

Listen to the dialogue and practice.

Officer: Welcome to Australia. May I see your passport, please?
Francesca: Yes. Here it is.
Officer: What is the purpose of your visit to Australia?
Francesca: I've come to study. I have a student visa.
Officer: So I see. And how long do you plan to stay?
Francesca: For one year.
Officer: Where will you be living?
Francesca: I'll be living in homestay accommodation with a host family.
Officer: I see. How are you going to get to your homestay from the airport?
Francesca: My school is picking me up.
Officer: OK. Enjoy your stay!
Francesca: Thank you.

Wordlist

- **purpose**
  What is the purpose of your visit to Australia?
- **homestay accommodation**
  I'll be living in homestay accommodation.
- **pick up**
  My school is picking me up.
- **vacancies**
  Do you have any vacancies?
- **single room**
  How much is a single room?
- **in advance**
  We ask for the full amount in advance.
- **complimentary breakfast**
  The price includes complimentary breakfast.
- **be served**
  Breakfast is served in the lobby.
- **check in**
  Is it too early to check in?
- **look after**
  We can look after your luggage for you.

Dialogue 2
Listen to the dialogue and practice.

Receptionist: Good morning. How can I help you?
Camilla: I'd like a single room. Do you have any vacancies?
Receptionist: Yes, we do. How long would you like to stay?
Camilla: Three nights. How much is a single room?
Receptionist: 150 dollars a night, and we ask for the full amount in advance. The price includes complimentary breakfast. Breakfast is served in the lobby between 7:30 am and 10 am.
Camilla: OK, I'll take it. Is it too early to check in?
Receptionist: I'm afraid you can't check in until 4 pm. We can look after your luggage for you until then, though.
Camilla: OK, that would be great. Thanks.
Receptionist: No problem. Now, if you could give me a credit card, I'll book you in.

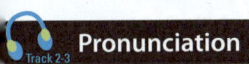
Pronunciation

Identifying Word Stress

Discover Pronunciation!

Listen again to the words from the lesson. Notice the way the speakers stress different syllables in the words. Practice saying the words, paying attention to the stressed syllables.

●	● ●	● ●	● ● ●	● ● ● ●	● ● ● ● ●	● ● ● ● ●
host	purpose	amount	vacancies	Australia	accommodation	complimentary
stay	visit		family			
price	lobby					

When you learn a new word, it is useful to learn which syllable is stressed. This will help you pronounce the word correctly.

Practice Pronunciation!

A Complete the sentences with words from the table above. Listen to check your answers. Then match the stress patterns with the words.

1. I'm afraid we don't have any ____ at the moment.
2. The price includes ____ internet access.
3. Are you going to stay with a ____ family?
4. Let's meet in the ____ at nine o'clock.
5. We can pay the full ____ in advance.

a. ● ●
b. ● ● ●
c. ● ●
d. ● ● ●
e. ● ● ● ● ●

B Practice saying the sentences in **A**. Pay attention to word stress.

Lesson 3: I'd like to rent a vehicle, please.

Dialogue 1
Listen to the dialogue and practice.

Attendant: Good morning, Madam. What can I do for you?
Rebecca: Good morning. I'd like to rent a vehicle, please.
Attendant: Certainly. What kind of vehicle would you like to rent?
Rebecca: I'd like an SUV. We are a large family.
Attendant: OK. Let me see. Yes, we do have an SUV available. It's a Chevrolet Traverse. Is that OK for you?
Rebecca: Yes, that will be fine. How much will it be?
Attendant: The fee is 75 dollars a day. The price includes fully comprehensive insurance, and unlimited mileage. How many days would you like the vehicle for?
Rebecca: I need it for seven days.
Attendant: OK, I can book that in for you now. Could I see your driver's license, please?
Rebecca: Yes. Here you are.
Attendant: Thank you. I'll also need a credit card to make the booking.
Rebecca: No problem. Thanks.

Wordlist

- **rent a vehicle**
  I'd like to rent a vehicle, please.

- **available**
  We do have an SUV available.

- **fully comprehensive insurance**
  The price includes fully comprehensive insurance.

- **unlimited mileage.**
  The price includes unlimited mileage.

- **make the booking**
  I'll also need a credit card to make the booking.

- **hire a car**
  We're going to hire a car and drive to San Diego.

- **pedestrian**
  If a pedestrian steps onto a crosswalk, you must stop.

- **disabled**
  Don't park in a disabled space!

- **pull over**
  If a police car follows you and flashes its lights, pull over.

- **offense**
  Drunk driving is a serious offense in the US.

Dialogue 2

Listen to the dialogue and practice.

Harry: Hey, Tae-young. I hear you're going on vacation next month. Where are you going?

Tae-young: Yes, that's right. Actually, I'm going to your home country, the US!

Harry: Wow, great! Whereabouts are you going?

Tae-young: I'm going to the west coast with my husband. We're going to hire a car and drive to San Diego, Phoenix, and Las Vegas.

Harry: Sounds fantastic!

Tae-young: Yes. I can't wait! Do you have any tips for driving in the US?

Harry: Sure. Firstly, remember that there is a 15 mph speed limit near schools. Also, if a pedestrian steps onto a crosswalk, you must stop and let them cross. And don't park in a disabled space! If you do, you will get a large fine.

Tae-young: Wow! There is a lot to remember.

Harry: Yes! Also, if a police car follows you and flashes its lights, pull over as soon as possible.

Tae-young: And then? Get out of the car?

Harry: No, you shouldn't get out of the car. You will need to show your driver's license to the police officer.

Tae-young: OK. Any other tips?

Harry: Yes. Never drink and drive! That is a serious offense in the US.

Pronunciation

Sentence Stress

Discover Pronunciation!

Listen to the extracts from **Dialogue 1** and **Dialogue 2**. Notice how the speaker stresses some words more than other words.

I'd like to rent a vehicle, please.

Wow! There is a lot to remember.

We stress important words (main verbs, nouns, adverbs, etc.) more than less important words (articles, auxiliary verbs, prepositions, pronouns, etc.).

Practice Pronunciation!

A Write the sentences in the correct columns. Then listen to check your answers.

> Close the window. Come to see me. What did you say?
> What's the time? Nice to meet you. Where did she go?

● ● ●	● ● ● ●	● ● ● ●

B Practice saying the sentences in **A** with your partner. Pay attention to sentence stress.

Lesson 4
What's your major?

Dialogue 1
Listen to the dialogue and practice.

Emily: Hello, look who's here! George Mason! What are you doing here? I thought you went to California.
George: Hi, Emily! I've been hoping to see you here. I got accepted by UCLA, but I received a scholarship from Arizona.
Emily: Great! That's why I chose this college, too. Otherwise, as an out-of-state student, I couldn't afford the tuition. So, what are you studying?
George: I'm studying chemistry. I'm thinking of going to medical school later on. How about you?
Emily: Well, I chose applied linguistics as my major. I'd love to teach English and other languages as a second language.
George: That sounds good. You speak English and Vietnamese. You'll make a great ESL teacher.
Emily: Thank you. I'm sure you will be a fine doctor, too.

Wordlist

- **get accepted**
  I got accepted by UCLA.

- **receive a scholarship**
  I received a scholarship from Arizona.

- **out-of-state**
  George is an out-of-state student. He's from Michigan.

- **afford the tuition**
  I can't afford the tuition at a private university.

- **applied linguistics**
  I chose applied linguistics as my major.

- **semester**
  I'm thinking of taking Dr Meyers's class next semester.

- **challenging**
  I heard her class is very challenging.

- **comforting**
  That's comforting to hear.

- **thorough**
  As long as you take thorough notes, you will be just fine.

- **sign up**
  I'm going to sign up for her class tomorrow.

Dialogue 2

Listen to the dialogue and practice.

Scott: Have you ever taken a class from Dr Meyers?
Ashley: Yes. As a matter of fact, she's my favorite lecturer. Are you going to take her class?
Scott: Yes, I'm thinking of taking her class next semester. I heard her class is very challenging, though.
Ashley: It's challenging for sure. I took about ten pages of notes in each of her classes. There was so much information!
Scott: Wow! That sounds like a lot of work. I'm looking for a really good lecturer.
Ashley: Well, then, Dr Meyers's class is the right class for you. She makes you work a lot, but she is also very understanding and kind.
Scott: That's comforting to hear. Did you find it difficult to get a good grade from her?
Ashley: She graded toughly, but I managed to get an A. As long as you focus on the lectures, do your reading assignments, and take thorough notes, you will be just fine.
Scott: Great. Thanks for your advice. I'm going to sign up for her class tomorrow.
Ashley: OK. Good luck! Enjoy your class!

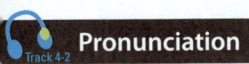

Pronunciation

Consonant Clusters

Discover Pronunciation!

Consonant clusters are groups of consonants that appear together in words.

Beginning Consonant Clusters

bl-	br-	cl-	cr-	dr-	fl-	fr-	gl-	gr-	pl-	pr-
sc-	sk-	sl-	sm-	sn-	sp-	squ-	st-	str-	sw-	tr-

Final Consonant Clusters

-ct	-ft	-lb, -lt	-mp	-nd	-ng
-nk	-nt	-pt	-sk	-sp	-st

Rare Clusters

shr- (shrink)	sph- (sphere)	thw- (thwart)

Practice Pronunciation!

A Listen to the words and practice saying them.

blame	**br**ain	**cl**ap	**cr**ab	**dr**ess
flood	**fr**og	**gl**ad	**gr**ab	**pl**an
prop	**sc**an	**sk**in	**sl**im	**sm**og
snap	**sp**an	**squ**are	**st**op	**str**eet
swim	**tr**ip	**tw**in	-	-

B Listen to the words and practice saying them.

blood **pr**essure	**cr**azy a**ct**	**sn**owstorm
clean **squ**are	**str**ange gi**ft**	e**st**ablished fa**ct**
slow ju**mp**	**fl**y **sk**y	**cl**ear **thr**oat

Lesson 4 • 17

Lesson 5: Do you want to live alone, or in a shared apartment?

Dialogue 1
Listen to the dialogue and practice.

Letting agent: So, how can I help you?
Jessica: I'm starting university here in September, so I'm looking for a place to live.
Letting agent: OK. Would you prefer a house, an apartment, or a student dormitory?
Jessica: I'd like an apartment.
Letting agent: I see. And, do you want to live alone, or in a shared apartment with a roommate?
Jessica: I think I'd prefer to live alone.
Letting agent: And what's most important to you: cost, location, or size?
Jessica: For me, location is the most important factor. I want to be close to the university.
Letting agent: I thought you would. We have a couple of one-bedroom apartments available in that area. The rent on both of them is 800 dollars a month. Would you like to take a look at them?
Jessica: Yes, please.

Wordlist

- **look for**
  I'm looking for a place to live.

- **dormitory**
  Would you prefer a house, or a student dormitory?

- **shared apartment**
  Do you want to live in a shared apartment with a roommate?

- **prefer**
  I think I'd prefer to live alone.

- **factor**
  For me, location is the most important factor.

- **rent**
  The rent on the apartment is 800 dollars a month.

- **take a look**
  Would you like to take a look at the apartments?

- **work overseas**
  I may have to go work overseas.

- **choice**
  I will have a choice between London and Madrid.

- **decision**
  This won't be an easy decision at all!

Dialogue 2

Listen to the dialogue and practice.

Judith: I was talking with my boss today. He said that within the next two years, I may have to go work overseas.
Rupert: Oh, really? Where will you go?
Judith: Well, I think I will have a choice between the London office and the Madrid office.
Rupert: Wow! I'd love to live in either of those cities. Which will you choose?
Judith: Well, I'm not sure. London may be better. I don't like hot weather, and Madrid is much hotter than London.
Rupert: Yes, but don't forget that it rains a lot more in London. Do you like rain?
Judith: No, of course I don't! I think London is a busier city than Madrid though. I like busy places.
Rupert: That may be true. But I heard that London is very expensive. Madrid is probably cheaper.
Judith: Good point. This won't be an easy decision at all!

Pronunciation

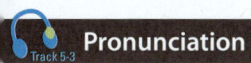

Sentence Stress: Unstressed Words

Discover Pronunciation!

Listen to the sentences. Notice how the speaker stresses some words more than other words.

Location	*or*	*size?* [conjunction]
Open	*the*	*window.* [article]
What's	*your*	*name?* [pronoun]
Go	*to*	*sleep!* [preposition]
I	*can*	*help.* [can]
She	*was*	*late.* [be]

We don't usually stress conjunctions, articles, pronouns, prepositions, or the verbs *can* and *be*.

Practice Pronunciation!

A Write the stress pattern for each sentence.

1. Close the door. ● • •
2. Where is John?
3. I want a house or an apartment.
4. How can I help you?
5. Give it to your teacher.

B Practice saying the sentences in **A** with your partner. Pay attention to sentence stress.

Lesson 6: That's quite a personal question.

Dialogue 1
Listen to the dialogue and practice.

Roy: Hello, I'm Roy. You must be Mia. Is this your first blind date?
Mia: Hi, Roy. Yes, it is. How about you?
Roy: Same here. So, what do you do for a living?
Mia: I'm a legal assistant at a law firm. And you?
Roy: I'm a computer programmer. I want to change jobs though. How much money do you make?
Mia: That's quite a personal question. Do you need a loan or something?
Roy: No offense. I was just curious. Anyway, I'm 28 years old. How old are you?
Mia: I'd rather not say. I'm old enough!
Roy: Actually, you look fairly young. Have you had plastic surgery?
Mia: Why? What's it to you?
Roy: Sounds like you have. Have you had liposuction, too?
Mia: That's a very rude question! Excuse me. I think I'd better get going.

Wordlist

- **blind date**
  Is this your first blind date?

- **for a living**
  What do you do for a living?

- **legal assistant**
  I'm a legal assistant at a law firm.

- **personal**
  That's quite a personal question.

- **curious**
  No offense. I was just curious.

- **plastic surgery**
  Have you had plastic surgery?

- **liposuction**
  Have you had liposuction, too?

- **rude**
  That's a very rude question!

- **apply**
  Actually, he suggested I apply to this company.

- **job-related**
  Could you ask me job-related questions, please?

Dialogue 2

Listen to the dialogue and practice.

Mr Jones: Come on in, Ms Evans. Have a seat.
Ms Evans: Thank you. It's nice to meet you, Mr Jones.
Mr Jones: Likewise. I saw you talking to Larry Parker just now. Do you know him?
Ms Evans: Yes, I do. Actually, he suggested I apply to this company.
Mr Jones: Really? Is he your boyfriend? You two seemed close.
Ms Evans: That's a bit personal, isn't it? If you don't mind, I'd rather not answer that question.
Mr Jones: All right. It's none of my business, I suppose. Are you available on weekends?
Ms Evans: Well, I prefer not to work on weekends. I need my own time.
Mr Jones: Are you married?
Ms Evans: That question makes me feel uncomfortable. Could you ask me job-related questions, please?

Pronunciation

Word Stress and Prefixes/Suffixes

Discover Pronunciation!

There are some rules to follow when we say words with prefixes or suffixes.

Prefixes (added at the beginning of words)

Verbs	**Short Prefixes** *dis-, un-, re-*, etc.	Do not stress the prefix. (It may have secondary stress.) repórt, discóver, refléct, uncóver
	Longer Prefixes *inter-, intro-, over-, under-, fore-*, etc.	Stress the verb or the root. The prefix has secondary stress. introdúce, foretéll, oversée, undertáke
Nouns	**Prefixes** *inter-, intro-, over-, tele-, fore-*, etc.	Stress the prefix. an ínterchange, fórehead, télevision

Suffixes (added to the end of words)

-eer, -ese, -ique, -ee	Primary stress **usually** falls on these suffixes Japanése, employée, uníque, voluntéer
-ial, -ual, -ian, -ion, -ious, -logy	Primary stress falls on the syllable in front of these suffixes musícian, anthropólogy, inféction, spécial
-ize, -ary, -ate, -ory	Primary stress falls two syllables before these suffixes drámatize, términate, sécondary, dórmitory
Other Suffixes	When suffixes are added to words, they usually keep the same stress as the word. wash + able = **wásh**able manage + er = **mán**ager delight + ful = **delíght**ful happy + ness = **háppi**ness

Lesson 7: What kind of treatment did you get?

Dialogue 1
Listen to the dialogue and practice.

Kate: Hi, Ron. What's the matter? You don't look well.
Ron: Hello, Kate. My shoulder and neck are killing me! They hurt so much, I can't do anything.
Kate: I know what you mean. I've had the same problem before. I had to get some treatment.
Ron: What kind of treatment did you get?
Kate: Well, I had a chiropractic adjustment. The doctor adjusted my spine and joints. After that, I felt much better.
Ron: Really? Did you hear a cracking sound during the treatment? I saw it on TV, and it scared me!
Kate: Oh, yes. I was very nervous at first. But once you get used to it, you learn to relax.
Ron: Maybe I should try it. Could you give me the doctor's phone number?
Kate: Sure, I'll give it to you now. The sooner you take care of it, the better.
Ron: Thank you so much, Kate. I'll treat you to lunch sometime!

Wordlist

- **hurt**
  They hurt so much, I can't do anything.
- **treatment**
  What kind of treatment did you get?
- **chiropractic adjustment**
  I had a chiropractic adjustment.
- **cracking sound**
  Did you hear a cracking sound during the treatment?
- **scare**
  I saw it on TV, and it scared me!
- **get used to**
  Once you get used to it, you learn to relax.
- **The sooner ... the better**
  The sooner you take care of it, the better.
- **fix**
  I've fixed you some ginger tea.
- **simmer**
  Let the tea simmer for about 15 to 20 minutes.
- **alternative medicine**
  There's both modern and alternative medicine.

Dialogue 2
Listen to the dialogue and practice.

Marie: Here you go, Kenny. I've fixed you some ginger tea.
Kenny: Ginger tea? Thank you. But why? What's it for?
Marie: It's for your cold. You've been coughing a lot. Ginger is especially good for colds and sore throats.
Kenny: I didn't know that. Let me have a taste. [pause] Yes, it's pretty good. How do you make it?
Marie: You boil some water and then add some ginger root. Let it simmer for about 15 to 20 minutes. Then add honey and lemon, if you want.
Kenny: That's pretty simple. People use so many different methods to stay healthy, don't they?
Marie: Yes, you're right. There's both modern and alternative medicine. When I have a headache, I get acupressure treatment instead of taking pills.
Kenny: That sounds interesting. Does it really work?
Marie: Yes, it does. It also has no side effects. You should give it a try.

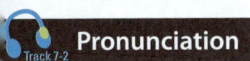

Pronunciation

Thought Groups and Intonation

Discover Pronunciation!

Thought groups are phrases that express separate ideas. Thought groups help listeners understand the meaning of a sentence.

Thought Groups and Grammatical Phrases
Grammatical phrases are often used as thought groups.

Prepositional Phrases	at the airport, at noon, in the classroom
Short Clauses	When you get there, call me. If you are thirsty, you can have some ice tea.
Verb + Pronoun/Noun	go swimming, get it, go home
Determiner + Noun	your dog, my phone, the car

Joining Thought Groups Together
We pause briefly after the last word in a thought group.

My friends ⇧ came over to the club house ⇧ for our science project.
     pause   pause

Thought Groups and Intonation
There is usually a small rise or fall at the end of a thought group.

My train ↗ is leaving ↗ at 9 o'clock. ↘
If you don't want to be late, ↗ we should start now. ↘

Practice Pronunciation!

Listen to the sentences and practice saying them.

1. She finished her English report.
2. I don't understand why they didn't support the President.
3. My sister and I went swimming at the community center yesterday.
4. Could you give me your dentist's phone number?
5. Boil some water and add some ginger root.

Lesson 8
What is an American wedding like?

Dialogue 1
Listen to the dialogue and practice.

Michelle: Wow, are these your wedding pictures? You look so beautiful!
Su-mi: Thank you. Our photographer captured our wedding perfectly.
Michelle: You are wearing different wedding dresses in the pictures. Did you have two wedding ceremonies?
Su-mi: No, we didn't. Nowadays many Korean weddings are a mixture of western and traditional styles. The bride and groom wear western clothes for the first part of the ceremony. Then, they change into traditional clothes for the second part.
Michelle: Traditional Korean clothes are so gorgeous! What did you do during the traditional part of the ceremony?
Su-mi: We took part in a custom called *pyebaek*. It's attended by family members only. During *pyebaek*, the bride formally greets her new parents-in-law.
Michelle: How interesting! In my country, the couple usually goes to a reception right after the ceremony. People give toasts to the couple and wish them happiness.
Su-mi: Would you like to attend a traditional Korean wedding ceremony? If you want, I'll take you to one.
Michelle: Really? That sounds terrific! It'll help me understand Korean culture much better.

Wordlist

- **capture**
  Our photographer captured our wedding perfectly.

- **ceremony**
  Did you have two wedding ceremonies?

- **bride and groom**
  The bride and groom wear western clothes for the ceremony.

- **gorgeous**
  Traditional Korean clothes are so gorgeous.

- **take part in**
  We took part in a custom called *pyebaek*.

- **give a toast**
  People give toasts to the couple and wish them happiness.

- **culture**
  It'll help me understand Korean culture much better.

- **get married**
  I hear your sister's getting married.

- **unique**
  Are there any unique traditions?

- **bridal shower**
  The maid of honor throws a bridal shower.

Dialogue 2 *Listen to the dialogue and practice.*

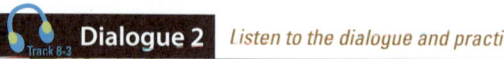

Akiko: Hello, Ryan! I hear your sister's getting married.
Ryan: Hi, Akiko. Yes, she's getting married in six weeks. She's going to send the wedding invitations soon. She'll send you one, too.
Akiko: I'll be happy to attend her wedding. What is an American wedding like? Are there any unique traditions?
Ryan: Well, before the wedding, the maid of honor throws a bridal shower. The bride-to-be receives gifts from her female friends.
Akiko: I see. What about the groom? Does he get anything from his friends?
Ryan: Actually, the groom hosts a bachelor party right before the wedding day. He and his male friends enjoy his last moments of freedom as a single man.
Akiko: Last moments of freedom? I think that's funny! OK, what else?
Ryan: Gifts are very important. People give gifts to the couple for their new home, or they give cash.
Akiko: In Japan, we don't bring gifts, but we do give money. We also pay an entrance fee to attend the wedding party.
Ryan: Really? I didn't know that. Well, you don't have to pay for the reception at my sister's wedding. Just come and have a good time!
Akiko: I sure will! I'll be looking forward to it.

Pronunciation

Rhythm Patterns

Discover Pronunciation!

Prepositions (Unstressed)
Short prepositions in prepositional phrases are not stressed.
*at **níght**, at **schóol**, for an **hóur***

Of
We usually pronounce *of* as /əv/. However, we sometimes pronounce it as /ə/ and we link the sound with surrounding sounds.
a cup of coffee → *a /**cuppə**/ coffee*
a couple of friends → *a /**coupələ**/ friends*

Separated Two-Word Verbs
We stress prepositions when they are part of a separated two-word verb.
*try them **ón**, finish it **óff**, look it **úp***

Practice Pronunciation!

Listen to the words and practice saying them.

1. bring them **back**
2. leave it **alone**
3. put the pictures **away**
4. fill it **out**
5. wake us **up**
6. turn the volume **down**
7. by **bus**
8. on **time**
9. at **home**
10. a **couple of** minutes
11. a **cup of** coffee
12. a **ton of** food

I ran a red light.

Dialogue 1
Listen to the dialogue and practice.

Steve: Guess what. I got a traffic ticket today.
Nicole: Really? What for?
Steve: For running a red light. I didn't notice that I did it. I heard a siren, and then I saw a police car flashing its lights behind me.
Nicole: So, what did you do?
Steve: I pulled over to the side of the road. The police officer got out of the car and told me I had run a red light.
Nicole: Did you tell him that you didn't know?
Steve: Yes, I did. I told him in a polite way. But he wrote me a ticket anyway.
Nicole: Couldn't he have just given you a warning? I got pulled over once, but I only got a warning.
Steve: Well, you did, but I didn't. This police officer went by the book. Now I have to go to court.
Nicole: Court? What's going to happen?
Steve: The judge will decide how much my fine will be.

Wordlist

- **traffic ticket**
  I got a traffic ticket today.

- **run a red light**
  I ran a red light and then saw a police car behind me.

- **pull over**
  I pulled over to the side of the road.

- **go by the book**
  The police officer went by the book.

- **fine**
  The judge will decide how much my fine will be.

- **robbery**
  Did you hear about the robbery at Central Bank?

- **be kidding**
  You've got to be kidding!

- **get down**
  Everybody get down on the floor!

- **panic**
  People panicked and just followed his instruction.

- **manage to**
  I managed to remember some things about them.

Dialogue 2 — Listen to the dialogue and practice.

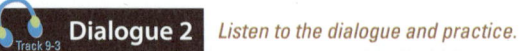

Kim: Dan, did you hear about the robbery at Central Bank?
Dan: Did I hear about it?! I was right there when it happened!
Kim: You've got to be kidding! Are you serious?
Dan: Yes, I'm serious. I was sitting on the couch waiting for my turn. All of a sudden, two men wearing masks came in. They were holding guns.
Kim: Oh my! Then what happened?
Dan: One of the guys shouted, 'Everybody get down on the floor!' People panicked and just followed his instruction.
Kim: Weren't you scared when you saw the guns?
Dan: I sure was. I tried not to look at the robbers. But I managed to remember some things about them.
Kim: Did you talk to the police about what you saw?
Dan: Yes, I did. I told them about the robbers' clothing and height, and about their weapons. I hope the police catch them soon.

Pronunciation

/s/ and /z/

Discover Pronunciation!

/s/ is voiceless. We make a sound like a snake: *Sssssssss*.

/z/ is voiced. We make a sound like a bee: *Zzzzzzzzzz*.

	/s/			/z/
s	yes, same, this		z	zoo, zebra, lazy
ss	asset, class, possible		zz	buzz, dizzy
se	course, promise, house		ze/se	size, wise
c	center, city, nice		s	busy, choose, please
sc	scene, science, scissors		ss	scissors, dessert
x	excellent, next, Texas		x	exam, exactly

Practice Pronunciation!
Listen and write /s/ or /z/ next to each word. Then practice saying the words.

1. crazy _____
2. civil _____
3. noise _____
4. choice _____
5. kiss _____
6. risen _____
7. talks _____
8. loose _____
9. reason _____
10. box _____
11. works _____
12. music _____
13. horse _____
14. choose _____
15. sings _____
16. easy _____

Lesson 10
What's your emergency?

Dialogue 1
Listen to the dialogue and practice.

Operator: What's your emergency?
Jennifer: It's a medical emergency! Help! I need an ambulance!
Operator: Calm down, please. Take a deep breath. What's the problem?
Jennifer: My husband collapsed. He's on the floor. He can't breathe!
Operator: Where are you now?
Jennifer: We're at home. The address is 2013 75th Place, Blooming Garden.
Operator: What's your name?
Jennifer: My name's Jennifer Gomez. Please, hurry!
Operator: Is your husband still conscious?
Jennifer: Yes, he is.
Operator: Is your front door unlocked? If not, could you unlock the door, please?
Jennifer: OK. I did it.
Operator: Good. Now stay on the line. I've dispatched an ambulance. It's on the way.

Wordlist

- **emergency**
  It's a medical emergency!

- **take a breath**
  Calm down, please. Take a deep breath.

- **collapsed**
  My husband collapsed. He's on the floor.

- **dispatch**
  I've dispatched an ambulance.

- **all of a sudden**
  All of a sudden, the fire alarm went off.

- **a close call**
  It was a close call.

- **fire drills**
  Thanks to the fire drills I practiced, I didn't panic.

- **be trapped in**
  She's trapped in her apartment!

- **climb up**
  There's a fire fighter climbing up the ladder.

- **prevention**
  Prevention is the best protection.

Dialogue 2

Listen to the dialogue and practice.

Pedro: Susan! Thank God you're safe! Are you OK?
Susan: Yes. I was just scared. I hope everyone got out of the building.
Pedro: I hope so, too. What happened? How did the fire start?
Susan: All of a sudden, the fire alarm went off. Then I heard people shouting 'fire' in the hallway.
Pedro: It was a close call. How did you manage to get out?
Susan: Thanks to the fire drills I practiced, I didn't panic. I got out of the apartment as quickly as possible.
Pedro: That's the most important thing. Look! There's a woman yelling out for help! She's trapped in her apartment!
Susan: There's a fire fighter climbing up the ladder. He's got her now. They're coming down together.
Pedro: Fires are so scary and dangerous. We should be careful all the time.
Susan: You're right. Prevention is the best protection.

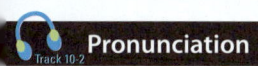

Pronunciation

Words Used as Nouns and Verbs

Discover Pronunciation!

Some words are nouns when they are stressed on the first syllable, and verbs when they are stressed on the second syllable.

Nouns		Verbs	
áddress	the place	*addréss*	to direct a speech
récord	a written official report	*recórd*	to set down in writing
défect	a shortcoming or fault	*deféct*	to desert one's country
présent	a gift	*presént*	to bring or give
súspect	a person who is suspected	*suspéct*	to doubt

Practice Pronunciation!

Listen to the words and practice saying them.

	Nouns	Verbs
❶	áddict	addíct
❷	rébel	rebél
❸	próduce	prodúce
❹	désert	desért
❺	pérmit	permít
❻	cónvert	convért
❼	óbject	objéct
❽	fínance	fináncé
❾	ínsult	insúlt
❿	cónvict	convíct

Lesson 11: What kind of job are you interested in?

Dialogue 1
Listen to the dialogue and practice.

Oscar: Hey, Penny. I thought I may run into you here. How's the job hunting going?

Penny: Not bad. I've talked with a few interesting employers here. How about you? What kind of job are you looking for?

Oscar: Well, I'm looking for a full-time job with good pay. I'd also like a job with a retirement plan and health insurance. That would be perfect! What kind of job are you interested in?

Penny: I want to work for a company that has good training programs. Then, when I'm older, I can go freelance using the skills I've learned. I don't want to be an office worker my whole life!

Oscar: Yes, I guess it would be nice to work freelance. That way you can be your own boss.

Penny: Exactly! Anyway, let's get on with our job hunting. See you later!

Oscar: Yes, and good luck!

Wordlist

- **job hunting**
  How's the job hunting going?
- **full-time job**
  I'm looking for a full-time job with good pay.
- **retirement plan**
  I'd also like a job with a retirement plan.
- **go/work freelance**
  I can go/work freelance using the skills I've learned.
- **get on with**
  Let's get on with our job hunting.
- **resume**
  Let's look at your resume in more detail.
- **editor**
  I've worked as an editor since I graduated.
- **mobile applications**
  I've worked on a number of web and mobile applications.
- **develop**
  I want to develop my skills in that area.
- **strength/weakness**
  What would you say are your strengths and weaknesses?

Dialogue 2
Listen to the dialogue and practice.

Ms Lee: Thank you for coming to today's interview, Paula.
Paula: It's a pleasure for me to be here. Thank you for inviting me.
Mr Jones: Let's start by looking at your resume in more detail. How long have you worked as an editor?
Paula: I've worked as an editor since I graduated. I've worked at Birdhouse Press for four years now.
Ms Lee: Do you have any experience of working on electronic products?
Paula: Yes, I do. I've worked on a number of web and mobile applications. That's why I want to work for your company. I want to work more on electronic products and develop my skills in that area.
Mr Jones: OK, good. And what would you say are your strengths and weaknesses?
Paula: I think my main strength is project management. As for my weakness ... I'm a perfectionist, so sometimes I don't know when to stop working on a project.

Pronunciation

Intonation in Questions

Discover Pronunciation!

Listen to the extracts from **Dialogue 2**. Notice how the speakers' voices rise or fall when they ask questions.

Mr Jones: *How long have you worked as an editor?* ↘
Paula: *I've worked as an editor since I graduated.*

Ms Lee: *Do you have any experience of working on electronic products?* ↗
Paula: *Yes, I do.*

When the answer to a question can be *yes* or *no*, the speaker's voice rises (↗). When the question is open, and *yes* or *no* cannot be the answer, the speaker's voice falls (↘).

Practice Pronunciation!

A Read the dialogue. Decide whether the speakers' voices should rise or fall after each question. Write ↗ or ↘ in each gap.

A: What kind of job are you looking for? ____
B: I'm looking for a job in a bank.

A: Do you want to work in a city? ____
B: Yes, I want to work in a city.

A: Do you have any experience of working in a bank? ____
B: Yes, I do.

A: How long have you worked in a bank? ____
B: Almost five years.

B Practice the dialogue in **A** with your partner, using your own personal information.

Lesson 12 — What do you enjoy about your job?

Dialogue 1
Listen to the dialogue and practice.

Penny: So, Oscar, how is your job going?
Oscar: Well, I still have a lot to learn, but I'm enjoying it.
Penny: What do you enjoy about it?
Oscar: I enjoy visiting clients. I like getting out of the office. I really dislike staying inside all day. What about you? Are you enjoying your job?
Penny: Well, I'm tired of going on business trips. Almost every week I go somewhere. I spent the last three weeks in Italy without a break. I'm exhausted!
Oscar: Yes, that sounds kind of extreme. Is there anything that you like about the job?
Penny: Yes, there are things that I like. I enjoy giving presentations. I also like attending meetings with co-workers from around the world. It's exciting and interesting.
Oscar: Yes, it must be. I try to avoid going to meetings in my company as they are kind of boring!

Wordlist

- **client**
  I enjoy visiting clients.

- **be tired of**
  I'm tired of going on business trips.

- **exhausted**
  I worked three weeks without a break. I'm exhausted!

- **extreme**
  That sounds kind of extreme.

- **give presentations**
  I enjoy giving presentations.

- **co-worker**
  I also like attending meetings with co-workers.

- **notice**
  I've noticed recently that you are often late for work.

- **luckily**
  Luckily, my wife picks my son up after school.

- **solution**
  That sounds like an excellent solution.

- **rush**
  You won't have to rush in the mornings.

Dialogue 2

Listen to the dialogue and practice.

Rachel: Greg, could I have a word with you? I need to talk to you about something.
Greg: Yes, of course.
Rachel: I've noticed recently that you are often late for work. Is there a reason why you can't get here on time?
Greg: I'm really sorry. The problem is that I have to take my son to school in the mornings. Sometimes when the traffic's bad, I just can't get here on time.
Rachel: I quite understand. I had the same problem when my kids were young. Do you pick your son up after school, too?
Greg: No. Luckily, my wife picks him up.
Rachel: Then how about this solution? Let's change your working hours to 9:30 to 5:30. That way you won't have to rush in the mornings, and you won't be late. Do you think that would help?
Greg: That sounds like an excellent solution. Thanks a lot for your understanding.
Rachel: No problem.

Pronunciation

-n't

Discover Pronunciation!

Listen to the sentences. Notice how the speaker stresses *can't*.

I **can** get here on time.   I **can't** get here on time.

Verbs with the negative ending *-n't* are always stressed, even when they are auxiliary verbs.

Practice Pronunciation!

A Listen and check (✓) the sentence that you hear, **a** or **b**.

1. ⓐ Are you free?   ⓑ Aren't you free?
2. ⓐ I can help you.   ⓑ I can't help you.
3. ⓐ We were happy.   ⓑ We weren't happy.
4. ⓐ She can swim.   ⓑ She can't swim.
5. ⓐ They were running.   ⓑ They weren't running.

B Practice saying the sentences in **A** with your partner. Does your partner know which sentence you are saying?

Lesson 13: I want to go somewhere special.

Dialogue 1
Listen to the dialogue and practice.

Sean: Marie, where do you want to go for our winter vacation?
Marie: Well, I want to go somewhere special, like the Ice Hotel in Sweden.
Sean: Ice Hotel? Are you saying it's made of real ice?
Marie: It sure is! It's made of snow and ice. It melts and turns into water in spring.
Sean: How interesting! Where can we sleep? In an ice room?!
Marie: Yes, actually! Guests sleep on beds built of snow and ice. We'll need to wear thermal underwear and a hat.
Sean: Amazing! How cold is the room?
Marie: They say it's about minus five degrees Celsius! Everything in the room, such as the furniture and sculptures, is made of ice.
Sean: It sounds so fascinating! Let's start planning our vacation right now.
Marie: Sounds good to me!

Wordlist

- **be made of**
  The Ice Hotel is made of snow and ice.

- **melt**
  It melts and turns into water in spring.

- **thermal underwear**
  We'll need to wear thermal underwear.

- **sculptures**
  The sculptures in the room are made of ice.

- **fascinating**
  It sounds so fascinating!

- **refreshed**
  You look very refreshed.

- **butler**
  We had a butler to assist us.

- **therapist**
  We had an in-house spa therapist!

- **cuisine**
  Did you have any traditional Balinese cuisine?

- **special package deal**
  The special package deal wasn't too expensive.

Dialogue 2
Listen to the dialogue and practice.

Steve: Hi, Angela! When did you get back from Bali?
Angela: Hey, Steve! I just got back yesterday.
Steve: You look very refreshed. How was the trip?
Angela: It was so wonderful! Our family rented a private villa. We had a private driver, a butler, a chef, and even an in-house spa therapist!
Steve: Wow! It sounds like a dream vacation!
Angela: That's not all. I swam in our private swimming pool and got beauty treatments everyday.
Steve: Sounds relaxing. How about the food? Did you have any traditional Balinese cuisine?
Angela: Of course I did. The chef cooked really delicious steamed rice, meat, and vegetables. She also made some western food.
Steve: I think my family would love to have a vacation like that. But wasn't it really expensive?
Angela: We went on a special package deal, so it wasn't too bad. If you're interested, I'll give you the information.
Steve: Yes, please. I'd appreciate that.

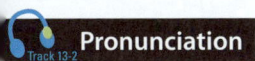

Pronunciation

/r/ and /l/

Discover Pronunciation!

When we pronounce /r/, the tip of the tongue curls back without touching the top of the mouth.

When we pronounce /l/, the tip of the tongue touches the top teeth.

Practice Pronunciation!

A Listen to the words and practice saying them.

1. rate / late
2. right / light
3. rice / lice
4. race / lace
5. berry / belly
6. pray / play
7. crash / clash
8. Rick / lick
9. correct / collect

B Practice saying the tongue twisters. Work with your partner.

1. Roberta ran rings around the Roman ruins.

2. Clean clams crammed in clean cans.

3. Luke Luck likes lakes.
   Luke's duck likes lakes.
   Luke Luck licks lakes.
   Luck's duck licks lakes.
   Duck takes licks in lakes Luke Luck likes.
   Luke Luck takes licks in lakes ducks like.

4. Lick the red lolly, lick the yellow lolly.
   Red lorry, yellow lorry.
   Laura and Larry rarely lull their rural roosters to sleep.
   Jerry's berry jelly really rankled his broiling belly.
   Collecting the corrections is the role of the elderly.

Lesson 14: I downloaded some apps for my smartphone.

Dialogue 1
Listen to the dialogue and practice.

Christina: Marco, you look so tired!
Marco: Yes, I've been up all night reading these books. I'm so worried about the exam next week. I always do so badly in exams!
Christina: Hmm … I think you need to practice your exam technique. Just studying books isn't enough.
Marco: Sure. But how can I do that?
Christina: Well, I downloaded some exam practice apps for my smartphone. With the apps, I can practice the exam with a timer, and also get tips on each question.
Marco: Wow, that sounds great! How can I get those apps?
Christina: First, go to the app store on your smartphone. Then, search for the name of the exam. When you see the exam apps, just press 'download'. That's it!
Marco: OK, I'll do that. Thanks for your advice, Christina.

Wordlist

- **be up all night**
  I've been up all night reading these books.

- **exam technique**
  I think you need to practice your exam technique.

- **download**
  I downloaded some apps for my smartphone.

- **get tips on**
  With the apps, I can get tips on each question.

- **contact**
  You can contact us whenever you need to.

- **show ... how to**
  I'll show you how to use it.

- **perfectly**
  I'm perfectly happy with our house phone.

- **charge up**
  You just charge the phone up every two days or so.

- **safe**
  We just want you to be safe.

- **concern**
  My biggest concern is your grandmother.

Dialogue 2
Listen to the dialogue and practice.

Hannah: Grandpa, why don't I buy you a cell phone? That way we can always contact you, and you can contact us whenever you need to.
Desmond: A cell phone?! No, thank you. I don't know how to use a cell phone.
Hannah: Cell phones are simple to use. I'll show you how to use it.
Desmond: I'm perfectly happy with our house phone. I don't need anything else.
Hannah: But, grandpa, the advantage of a cell phone is that you can take it with you wherever you go.
Desmond: But doesn't it use a lot of electricity?
Hannah: No. You just charge the phone up every two days or so. Then you can take it with you when you go out. That's why I think you should have a cell phone.
Desmond: I don't need to contact anyone when I go out!
Hannah: Oh, grandpa. We just want you to be safe. Cell phones are useful for staying in touch when you go out.
Desmond: I know. Thank you, dear. But my biggest concern is that your grandmother would be able to call me wherever I am!
Hannah: Well, that's a good point!

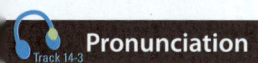
Pronunciation

Exclamations

Discover Pronunciation!

Listen to the extracts from **Dialogue 1** and **Dialogue 2**.

Marco, you look so tired!
I always do so badly in exams!
Wow, that sounds great!
I don't need to contact anyone when I go out!
Well, that's a good point!

When we make exclamations (!), our intonation rises.

Practice Pronunciation!

Practice saying the sentences with your partner.

1. Look out!
2. You look fantastic!
3. That's my pen!
4. Oh no!
5. This is a disaster!

Lesson 15
I'm against the idea.

Dialogue 1
Listen to the dialogue and practice.

Jack: Kate, I'm so hungry. Let's go to Super Burger.
Kate: You want a hamburger? In that case, no thanks. I don't eat fast food.
Jack: You don't? How come? I love hamburgers with French fries. There's nothing like fast food when you don't have much time.
Kate: Yes, but it's so unhealthy. It contains a lot of fat, salt, and calories.
Jack: Yes, that's true, but as long as you don't eat it everyday, you'll be fine.
Kate: I don't agree. Fast food will make you put on weight. Then you'll get high blood pressure and heart problems.
Jack: I see what you mean, but that's not a problem for me. I exercise regularly. I like fast food because it saves time and money.
Kate: I take your point, but you still need to be careful with fast food.
Jack: You could be right. I think I'll eat less fast food from now on. And I'll eat salads for lunch.
Kate: Sounds great. Then I will come with you for lunch!

Wordlist

- **in that case**
  You want a hamburger? In that case, no thanks.
- **contains**
  Fast food contains a lot of fat, salt, and calories.
- **As long as**
  As long as you don't eat it everyday, you'll be fine.
- **put on weight**
  Fast food will make you put on weight.
- **blood pressure**
  You'll get high blood pressure and heart problems.
- **regularly**
  I exercise regularly.
- **I take your point**
  I take your point, but you still need to be careful.
- **from now on**
  I think I'll eat less fast food from now on.
- **against the idea**
  I'm against the idea for a few reasons.
- **ride**
  I don't want to worry about the weather and the long ride.

Dialogue 2

Listen to the dialogue and practice.

Jenny: Miguel, I've been thinking about our plan to go to the Grand Canyon. I think we'd better change the plan.
Miguel: You were all for the idea until last night! What changed your mind?
Jenny: Well, I'm against the idea for a few reasons. First of all, we're planning to stay in a hotel in Phoenix, right? It's going to be very hot.
Miguel: Yes, but we'll leave for the Grand Canyon early in the morning and come back in the evening. The Grand Canyon isn't so hot.
Jenny: Yes, that's quite true, but it'll take about four hours to get there from the hotel. We'll be exhausted. I think we should go to Hawaii. In Hawaii, you walk out of the hotel, and you're on the beach.
Miguel: I agree, but we can't afford a trip to Hawaii. The flights and hotels would be much more expensive.
Jenny: You're right, but it's our vacation. I'd like to relax and enjoy the trip. I don't want to worry about the weather and the long ride.
Miguel: All right. Let's check on special deals on Hawaiian vacation packages. Then we can decide what to do.
Jenny: Agreed. Thank you. You're so sweet.

Pronunciation

Can and Can't

Discover Pronunciation!

Can	Can't
• Usually the vowel is not pronounced. It sounds like the ending of chi<u>cken</u>. *I can [ken] dance..* • In short answers, can is stressed. *Yes, I can [kæn].*	• The vowel is stressed and pronounced strongly and clearly. *I can't [kænt] dance.*

Practice Pronunciation!

Practice singing the song. Pay attention to your pronunciation of *can* and *can't*.

There's nothing you **can** do that **can't** be done.
Nothing you **can** sing that **can't** be sung.
Nothing you **can** say but you **can** learn how to play the game.
It's easy.

Nothing you **can** make that **can't** be made.
No one you **can** save that **can't** be saved.
Nothing you **can** do but you **can** learn how to be you in time.
It's easy.
All you need is love.

Lesson 16: I'd probably ask him for his autograph.

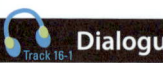

Dialogue 1
Listen to the dialogue and practice.

Paul: Guess what! Yesterday I met Tony Jackson!
Jenny: You mean Tony Jackson, the actor? Wow! Where did you meet him?
Paul: He came to my company's anniversary party.
Jenny: Oh, I see. So what did you say to him?
Paul: Actually, I didn't say anything. I didn't know what to say to him!
Jenny: Oh, so you didn't actually *meet* him!
Paul: Well … I guess not. Have you ever met a celebrity?
Jenny: No, I haven't.
Paul: What would you do if you did?
Jenny: I'd probably ask him for his autograph. But, if I met Tony Jackson …
Paul: Yes? What would you have done if you were me?
Jenny: I'd have taken a photo with him. He's so handsome!
Paul: Whatever!

Wordlist

- **anniversary**
  Tony Jackson came to my company's anniversary party.
- **actually**
  Actually, I didn't say anything. I didn't know what to say to him!
- **celebrity**
  Have you ever met a celebrity?
- **autograph**
  If I met a celebrity, I'd probably ask him for his autograph.
- **sunset**
  Sunset always makes me think of the future.
- **dream of**
  I've always dreamt of traveling.
- **earn**
  I'm going to get a part-time job to earn some money.
- **graduate**
  I'm planning to study law at graduate school.
- **get married**
  I hope to get married and start a family someday.
- **ahead of**
  We have our whole lives ahead of us.

Dialogue 2

Listen to the dialogue and practice.

Jason: Sunset always makes me think of the future.
Raquel: Me too. Summer's almost over. What are your plans for the future?
Jason: I'm planning to apply to graduate school next year. How about you?
Raquel: Well, I've always dreamt of traveling. I'm going to get a part-time job in the fall to earn some money.
Jason: Sounds good. I'd like to travel, too, but I think I should study more first. I hope to start my own company before I'm 30.
Raquel: My hope is to become a lawyer. I'm planning to study law at graduate school in a few years' time.
Jason: Cool. Do you have any other dreams?
Raquel: Well, I hope to get married and start a family someday.
Jason: Me too. It's exciting, isn't it? We have our whole lives ahead of us.
Raquel: Right. Let's meet here again someday and see how our lives have changed.
Jason: It's a deal!

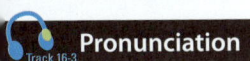

Pronunciation

Pronoun Contractions

Discover Pronunciation!

Listen to the extracts from **Dialogue 1** and **Dialogue 2**. Notice how the speakers say the highlighted words.

I'd probably ask him.

I'm planning to apply.

I've always dreamt of traveling.

I'm going to get a part-time job.

I'd like to travel.

We do not usually stress pronouns or pronoun contractions.

Practice Pronunciation!

A Underline the stressed words in each sentence.

① I've finished it.
② I'll ask him.
③ He's seen her.
④ We've done it.
⑤ She'd help him.

B Practice saying the sentences in **A**. Pay attention to stress.

NOTES

NOTES

NOTES